Radiant & Redeemed

Rediscovering Purity in a Culture of Chaos

Kate Leverett

RADIANCE PRESS
— LLC —

Scripture quotations taken from the New American Standard Bible®, Copyright © 1960, 1962, 1963, 1968, 1971, 1972, 1973, 1975, 1977, 1995 by The Lockman Foundation. Used by permission. (www.Lockman.org)

Editor: Megan Tatreau

Published by Radiance Press LLC

Printed in the United States of America

Paperback ISBN: 979-8-9904007-0-2
DIGITAL Edition ISBN: 979-8-9904007-1-9

Cover design by David Provolo

For more information visit kateleverett.com

Table of Contents

Dedication and Gratitude

This book is dedicated to my Mom
who devoted her life to embodying
the Christ-like example for others.

A special thanks to my husband, Brian,
and Katie for their consistent support
and guidance throughout this journey.
There aren't enough Diet Cokes and
Dr. Peppers in the world to express
my gratitude for all you've done!

Preface

I am absolutely passionate about purity! It's my favorite topic to teach on, and here is why: how you respond to purity NOW will impact you for the rest of your life! Take just a minute to let that sink in. The ways in which you react to purity now will forever leave an imprint on you, whether positive or negative. In the United States, we've seen alarming increases in the last decade of anxiety, depression, and non-suicidal self-injury among teen girls. Many adolescent females are seeking fulfillment through their relationships from the created rather than the Creator. We're no longer looking to God's Word as our guide on purity. Rather than striving for holiness, we've almost completely conformed to the world. It's time to stand up! I owe it to my children. You owe it to your children. It's time to rediscover purity through the lens of our Creator!

During the course of this book, I hope to provide you with some of the knowledge I've gained about purity that I wish my mom would have shared with me when I was an early teen. My mom even waited to give me the *All About Your Body* book until I was eighteen and headed off to Faulkner for college. I was like, "'Really Mom???!" Obviously, my parents weren't comfortable talking about purity. So what did that mean for me? It meant I gained a lot of my learning on purity on my own because my parents did not feel comfortable sharing those crucial, intimate conversations with me. I could have avoided so many mistakes along the way if they would have faced the difficult conversations about purity. So, as uncomfortable and awkward as it can be at times, I'm not taking that approach with my own children. I'm having discussions on purity! I don't want my kids to experience learning the same way I did, and I don't want that for you, either.

One of my primary goals in addressing this topic is for you to recognize that purity is a process. It does not happen instantaneously! As you grow and mature in your spiritual walk, your ideas on purity will shift. I'll share some of my personal stories of how that has happened in my life throughout the book. I hope this book will challenge, encourage, and renew your desire to live a Radiant and Redeemed life for God.

Expressive Writing: It's Your Turn!

My earnest desire in writing this book is to do everything within my power to help you grow in your walk with Christ. Journaling as a method of personal reflection is a phenomenal method to extend and stretch your faith. I encourage you to purchase a journal, or use whatever electronic method you prefer, to begin reflecting on your own personal journey throughout purity. Start this journey by defining what purity means to you. See how this changes as you complete the book.

Chapter 1

Defining Purity

"Mommy, how are kids made? Doesn't it happen
when you kiss your husband?"

I love car ride conversations with my kiddos! For starters, I don't have to look at them when I'm discussing awkward topics of conversation. More importantly, though, I love to hear the innocence—the sweet, pure thoughts of young children. As kids grow up, that innocence we cherish so much can come under attack from the world and everything in it. So, what exactly is purity, why do we value it, and how do we protect it? Purity is defined as "freedom from anything that debases, contaminates, pollutes; freedom from guilt or evil, innocence; virginity."[1] In the Bible, purity is often associated with chasteness and being found blameless before God. In Matthew 5:8, we are told, "Blessed are the pure in heart, for they will see God." As Christians, we need to have a heart that shows through our actions that we are fully committed to God. We should strive to live in such a way that reflects our faith and dedication to God. Jesus loves the purity and innocence of His children, just as I enjoy these qualities in mine. In Matthew 19:14, it says, "the kingdom of heaven belongs to such as these."

Expensive Utensils or Disposable Dinnerware

Did you know that before you were even created, God had a purpose for you? I find such comfort in the inspired words God recorded in Jeremiah 29:11:

> "'For I know the plans that I have for you,' declares the Lord, 'plans for prosperity and not for disaster, to give you a future and a hope.'"

Living in a world of over eight billion people, it's easy to feel insignificant, as if our day-to-day lives aren't worth much.[2] But God has a purpose for you in His redeeming plan for humanity! He wants you to be part of His story, but you have to decide how your piece will fit into the puzzle. You will have to determine if you want to live a life that demonstrates God is worth everything to you.

Second Timothy 2:20-21 provides a beautiful representation of the immeasurable value you have to God.

> "Now in a large house there are not only gold and silver implements, but also implements of wood and of earthenware, and some are for honor while others are for dishonor. Therefore, if anyone cleanses himself from these things, he will be an implement for honor, sanctified, useful to the Master, prepared for every good work."

In the first century, gold and silver were the most valuable and desirable vessels, reserved for special events. Clay and wood held much less value, being used as everyday materials. God's desire is for us to be the priceless utensil made of gold and silver designed to be used for extraordinary purposes. As Christians, we must choose to be either expensive utensils or disposable dinnerware. You were not made to be something cheap, worthless, and easily thrown away. God created you for something far greater, but many times, the way we dress and react to our peers at school, and our apathy towards obedience to God, is much more representative of disposable silverware. It's too easy to be lazy and just go with the flow. We want to fit in with our friends, we're scared to look "weird," and we certainly don't want to give up our popularity. We become more consumed by what others think of us than the value we have to God. *We are, in essence, selling our purity for cheap plasticware.*

More than Sex

When you consider physical cleanliness, one item you use daily to keep yourself clean is your toothbrush. Can you imagine using your toothbrush for anything other than its intended purpose? The very thought of taking that clean, bright-white toothbrush and using it to polish your nails or car and then resuming teeth brushing is, well, repulsive. Sometimes we put impure things into our minds, hearts, and even our physical bodies and do more harm than a dirty toothbrush would. Yet, with something as simple as a toothbrush, we'd never allow it to happen. Why do we do that? Because we have a lack of understanding of all that purity encompasses. In addition, many of us fail to grasp how the "little things" we allow into our hearts and minds could affect our purity and relationship with Christ, costing us everything.

In Ephesians 5:3-5, we gain an understanding of what God wants for His people as it relates to purity. It states,

> "But sexual immorality or any impurity or greed must not even be mentioned among you, as is proper among saints; and there must be no filthiness or foolish talk, or vulgar joking, which are not fitting, but rather giving of thanks. For this you know with certainty, that no sexually immoral or impure or greedy person, which amounts to an idolater, has an inheritance in the kingdom of Christ and God."

When you search YouTube or Google with the keyword "purity," a vast majority of the results all reference one word, *sex*. When I've heard lessons on purity using this text, it's been an almost verbatim repetition of the internet search results: sex was the primary aspect addressed. However, this passage extends far beyond abstaining from sex outside of marriage. It includes *any kind* of impurity. Our dating relationships, friendships, entertainment choices, morals, cultural values, personal identity, appearance, and even technology can influence our purity.

Journey to Holiness: Redefine Your Value

As Christians, we should be leading the charge for purity in every aspect of our lives. We are called to be a light in a world of darkness. We are told to be "imitators of God" (Ephesians 5:1). How do we imitate Christ? We get up every day and do our best to live a pure and righteous life for God. We find our value not by the number of likes on Instagram but rather by being the daughter of the King. We develop dating relationships aimed towards God instead of pursuing those that take advantage of our personal insecurities. We dress in a way that displays our dignity and respect as being a child of God instead of wearing clothes that merely make us *feel* beautiful. If you aren't striving to live a pure and righteous life, you aren't ready to fulfill the purpose God has for you. His desire is that you'll pursue holiness and a close relationship with Him over everything else in your life. Are you going to fail? Absolutely! But that doesn't relinquish you from your responsibility of trying. God's desire is for you to be an example to your family, your friends, and everyone you meet.

It's easy as a Christian teen living in a culture consumed with self-gratification to start believing life should be more about your personal journey to happiness and less about God's holiness. We tend to have a "What's in it for me?" mentality, but don't be disillusioned by what culture is projecting to you. We are told to "set your minds on the things that are above" (Colossians 3:2). We need to be more concerned about God's holiness and being a part of His redeeming plan than indulging in our own personal fulfillment. Instead of worrying about what you'll miss out on if you say no to watching an R-rated movie with your friends or how embarrassed you'll feel if you wear athletic attire that doesn't look like everyone around you, ask yourself, "Is God worthy of my purity?" Is the Creator of this universe—the One who knew me before I was even born, the One who was willing to go to the cross for me—is He worth it? Once you start defining your value by what God sees instead of the world's perspective, you will experience freedom! You'll never be good enough if you settle for the world's standards. You've got to start believing that God knows you better than your friends know you. You are worthy because of Whose you are, not because of how you want to be perceived.

"But you are a chosen people, a royal priesthood, a holy nation, a people for *God's* own possession, so that you may proclaim the excellencies of Him who has called you out of darkness into His marvelous light" (1 Peter 2:9).

So, what is your future in God's story? God has amazing plans for your life. He will use you if you let Him. God's desire is that we give up everything to fulfill His ministry. Luke 14:33 says, "Any of you who does not give up everything, he cannot be my disciple." Is He worthy to you? He wants you to pursue Him, love Him, and be willing to give up your worldly desires and replace them with His plan for your life.

It's Time for Reflection!

1. As we contemplate purity, take a moment to reflect on the areas of purity you struggle with the most. Search deep in your heart and identify the things you need to give up to seek the Kingdom of Heaven (Matthew 6:33).

2. What's holding you back in your pursuit of purity with Christ? Remember, if you aren't striving for purity, you aren't ready to carry out the plan God has for your life. God wants you to stop acting like cheap dinnerware and instead, be used as the vessel of honor at the King's table.

3. What is something impure in your life that you need to give up in order to pursue purity? Take this time to journal about it now and pray about it every day this week!

Chapter 2

Building Your Circle

♥ ♥ ♥ ♥ ♥ ♥ ♥ ♥ ♥ ♥ ♥ ♥ ♥ ♥ ♥ ♥

O ur friendship began in 1998 on a hot summer day down an old dusty road in Hahira, Georgia. I was fourteen and didn't like bugs, snakes, or anything remotely dirty. I came fully-loaded on that Sunday in June with enough Lysol to clear the Sahara Desert and a Caboodle full of hair-care products, curling irons, and make-up—I was totally prepared for a week of camp! Then I met Katie. City girl meets country girl (and an all-star athlete as well). I'm pretty sure she didn't realize what she'd gotten herself into when she found out she was going to be in Cabin Tyre with me that week! That, my friends, was the start to a lifetime of friendship!

Four years later, we decided to become college roommates. Katie got me through some of the most awkward, heart-wrenching, fun, and disappointing years of my life. We shared our latest crushes, played intramural sports together, took too many road trips to count, and participated in numerous spiritual conversations during our years at Faulkner. Twenty years later, I couldn't ask for a more loyal sister in Christ. We've laughed together as we reminisced about our college shenanigans and cried together during the lowest parts of our lives when we've lost mutual friends and family.

I hope you have a "Katie" in your life! Friendships are incredibly important during your adolescent years and are a major part of forming your sense of identity outside of your family. We tend to pick our friends by external factors, such as how they look, how they act, or if you share mutual interests. Although it's not unreasonable to want to share some of the same interests, the Christian attributes of a friend should be much more important! Christian friendships support the development of empathy and compassion. These friends give you a sense of belonging and acceptance. Christian friends are honest, trustworthy, loyal, and supportive, especially of your spiritual goals/attributes. Jonathan and David are a famous set of friends that represent the blessing of spiritual friendships. In 1 Samuel 18:1, it says, "Jonathan committed himself to David, and Jonathan loved him as himself."

Worldly friendships can look much different. Often, the identity of a worldly friendship is, "I'll do something for you only if you'll do something for me" or "I'll act like your friend to your face but will secretly talk badly about you behind your back." This mindset will lead you to friends who are selfish, manipulative, and temperamental. These qualities of a friend are contradictory to the identity of friendship in God's Word. Second Corinthians 6:14 reminds us, "Do not be mismatched with unbelievers; for what do righteousness and lawlessness share together, or what does light have in common with darkness?" Christians should build their strongest connections with other like-minded individuals who share Jesus' values and mission.

I recently ran across this thought:

*In Mark 2, Jesus healed a paralyzed man because
of his friends' faith. This is why your circle matters.[1]
~Kevin Jackson*

Can this be said of your circle? Does it really matter? Absolutely it does! The friends you pick will have a powerful influence on your life! Your circle will either strengthen your relationship with Christ or lead you further down the path of sin. You need deep spiritual friendships with other Christian women who will walk beside you. These people should be your Christian community, individuals in your life who not only love and support you but also hold you accountable. True sisters in Christ will share what we need to hear rather than what we want to hear. These women will pray for us and help us walk with the Lord. Can this be said of your closest friends? What can we learn about your circle from a quick glance at your friends' social media accounts? Are your friends inclusive of others or would they be better described as trolls on social media, maliciously hurting others? Are they careful about posting things that may cause others to stumble or do they blatantly share inappropriate pictures of things you know God would condemn? We have all heard that "bad company corrupts good morals" (1 Corinthians 15:33), but many times our actions suggest we don't believe it. Too many teenagers attempt to justify their close friendships with those who drink alcohol, curse, and have little desire for living a faithful life to God by arguing that Jesus hung out with sinners, too. But Jesus' entire mission was to bring people into repentance so they could be saved. He did not become all things to all people by sharing a beer with them, belittling others, or blending in *a little too well* with the world. The very thought contradicts James 4:4, which states, "whoever wants to be a friend of the world makes himself an enemy of God." Instead, Jesus desires for you to develop relationships that will lead you to Heaven.

Breaking Down Barriers and Building Bonds

So, how do we form a bond with our sisters that allows us to be vulnerable and share our personal struggles? How do we develop spiritual friendships over worldly ones? First of all, we have to put ourselves in a position to meet like-minded teens! While you may meet some Christian teens at school, becoming involved in a church youth group or something similar is the best way to connect with those who share your faith. We have to put down our phones and spend time face-to-face participating in social and spiritual activities through camps, devotionals, and youth group outings. I had several godly friends who were slightly older than me in high school, and they were crucial to staying true to myself and God. These women were a true blessing in my life! It is critical that you develop relationships with your Christian sisters who are going through or have been through many of the same trials and temptations you are facing or will face so that they can be a support for you, too.

What we learn when we begin to open up about our personal struggles is that fleshly desires are similar among all of us. "Their life is better than mine…" "They have way more friends than I do…" "They don't have struggles like I do." These thoughts are totally wrong! Don't buy into them! When's the last time you got on social media and posted a negative reel of your life, times when you failed God and appeared much more like cheap plasticware than fine china? Probably never! And your friends haven't either. We only share the good stuff. Now, I'm not saying to get out there and "tell all" about your life on social media. There's a better venue for that. What I am telling you is that you need to develop the kind of relationship with your Christian sisters that allows you to share the most intimate struggles with them. You can use your personal experiences to help others grow. Maybe you've learned how to overcome feelings of guilt related to your own past mistakes, so you can teach someone else who is struggling with similar thoughts. Healing begins when we share our experiences and lean on our Chrisitan community.

I've found, in ministering to women of all ages, that many are apprehensive about developing close, personal friendships with their sisters in Christ. Personal insecurities, feeling alone, fear of comparison, and even fear of gossip cause many to maintain superficial relationships in their circle. Although some negative emotions derive from our own false perception of others, things like gossip and comparison are justifiable reasons for apprehension.

Here's a recent example in my life. Not long ago, two teen girls visited our church for a youth event. As I sat a row behind them, I quickly realized they were laughing about another girl's appearance. How very sad! The quote, *"Confidence is silent. Insecurities are loud,"* [2] explains these girls' actions well. I hope your inner circle is not representative of these two girls. When we lack self-confidence, we tend to become jealous and demonstrate our insecurities by comparing, talking negatively, and rejecting others. This is why *"What Susie says of Sally says more of Susie than of Sally."* [3] You can learn a lot about a person by simply listening to what they say about others. Are your closest friends quick to criticize someone else or are they known for the encouragement they bring to other people's lives? **Remember, how we treat other people is a direct reflection of how we feel about ourselves and the type of friend we really are.**

Being the Right Friend

Equally as important as *finding* the right friend is *being* the right friend. People are drawn to others who are similar to themselves. If your personal standard is to demonstrate Christ-like characteristics, and you embody becoming the friend you desire to find, you're going to set yourself up for developing strong, spiritual friendships. Katie has been a friend who embodies godly characteristics to me. Here are some practical ways you can be a "Katie" to others in your life:

❀ A good friend treats everyone with kindness and respect, regardless of how they look or how they act. Use your friendships to "encourage one another and build one another up" (1 Thessalonians 5:11). Make every person feel valued and included. If you treat others with compassion and kindness, you'll likely attract those who do the same.

❀ A good friend will tell you the truth, even when it's difficult to hear. We all need friends who are more concerned about our heavenly future than our earthly happiness. Be a friend who *gently* shares the truth when your friends need it (Galatians 6:1).

❀ A friend of God leaves room for others to join their inner circle (Romans 15:7). Seek opportunities to bring others into your circle. God will continue to bring new people into your life to help you reach your spiritual goals if you'll let Him.

❀ A good friend is not a fair-weather friend. They are "devoted to one another in brotherly love" (Romans 12:10). They don't leave you hanging when someone with a little more swag comes around. Be a friend to others no matter the circumstances.

❀ A godly friend will willingly carry your burdens with you (Galatians 6:2). Be willing to share the struggles of your Christian sisters. Pray for and encourage them.

❀ A Christian friend will walk through the darkest part of your life with you. When you feel like you've disappointed God to a point of no return, they'll be there to give you the motivation you need to start walking with God again. Ecclesiastes 4:9-10 tells us, "Two are better than one because they have a good return for their labor; for if either of them falls, the one will lift up his companion. But woe to the one who falls when there is not another to lift him up!" This is one of the greatest gifts you can give to any of your friends.

❀ A good friend is a spiritually minded individual. They take every opportunity to influence others for Jesus. Their love for

Jesus inspires others to share the gospel, too! Be the light to every-one around you (Matthew 5:14). Your influence is powerful.

You will find that the path to purity will be a lot less bumpy if your inner circle is composed of Christian sisters. Heaven is much more attainable when you develop friendships with those who encourage you, share your burdens, and have the mutual goal of Heaven. Develop those relationships! It will be a blessing to you both.

It's Time for Reflection!

1. Take some time this week to reflect on your inner circle. Who are they? Are they your spiritual sisters in Christ who are walking with you down the path to Heaven?

2. Identify some girls you would like to develop closer relation-ships with, who would encourage you to pursue Christ with greater passion.

3. Pick one of these peers to begin building a closer relation-ship with this week. The path to relationship building can be as simple or as extravagant as you want. Start by sending an occasional funny meme or your favorite video clips, or go grab ice cream together. Do something to let her know you care about and appreciate her as your Christian sister. See if it doesn't make a difference in bringing you closer together with each other and in Christ.

Chapter 3

Recognizing Your Worth

I was roughly nine years old when my grandmother asked me to hop onto the scale. I was in no way overweight, more likely underweight. I still vividly remember walking into the bathroom of her double-wide trailer where she proudly kept that tall white and black scale. Once I told her my weight, my grandmother quickly responded, "Well, you better be careful, so you don't get fat like your Mom." I'm fairly certain my grandmother suffered from mental health issues. Unfortunately, one of those issues was an unhealthy fixation on weight and looks. She had a magic number she deemed the "fat weight," and during my most impressionable years, I found myself constantly worrying about staying underneath that number. I did crunches at night, worked out a lot, and was very careful to eat low-fat or no-fat foods, which probably weren't good for me, anyway. When I looked in the mirror, all I could see was a little bit of "pudge" and was disgusted by it. I rarely felt good about how I looked; my flaws always stuck out. My grandma grew up in a time when women gained much of their personal value based on how they looked and presented themselves to others. She had no idea a few comments would cause mental battles I still have to fight thirty years later.

Maybe you don't have a grandmother who made you get on the scale, but in a society where 80 percent of girls have been on a diet by age ten and 78 percent identify as being unhappy with their bodies by eighteen, I suspect you can relate.[1] There are so many things that affect our identity and self-worth. These include the number on the scale, the grade on your assignment, negative self-talk, your family relationships, how your inner circle treats you, and the influence of social media, just to name a few.

We have so many external pressures to look or be a certain way. I'd guess, from what I've found in my own research, that the number one factor influencing the self-worth of teen girls is social media. There's actually science linked to the feelings of anxiousness and depression we experience as a result of obsessive social media use (check out Chapter six for more!). It's no surprise that teens around the US are struggling with low self-esteem when social media offers attractive facial filters and editing apps designed to remove imperfections and enhance your looks with an easy tap and swipe. You might have felt confident in your appearance until that Snapchat filter uncovered what you could look like with no scars or blemishes and a toned body.

A recent report from the University of London on how people use social media found that 90 percent of the young women in the study said they used filters or edited their photos to do things like "reshape their jaw or nose, shave off weight, brighten or bronze skin, and whiten teeth."[2] When asked about the impact of social media, "90% of participants felt pressure to look attractive, 70% felt pressure to showcase a perfect life, and over 75% said they would 'never live up to the images you see.'"[3] Is it any wonder that about one in fifty people now have body dysmorphic disorder, a body image disorder where those who struggle with it can spend hours each day obsessing over imagined flaws or a slight imperfection in their appearance?[4]

Taking Off Our Capes

I listened to a powerful Ted Talk called "Lessons from the Mental Hospital" about a woman named Glennon Melton who had struggled with addiction for over eighteen years. During the YouTube video, Glennon shared how difficult it was for her to express her true self to others: "I started to feel like a loser in a world that prefers superheroes. So, I made my own capes and tied them tight around me. For eighteen years, my capes of pretending and addiction kept me safe and hidden…In high school, pretending was a matter of survival. We acted tough when scared or confident when confused."[5] Maybe you haven't put on the cape of addiction, but are there other capes you've worn? Have you put on a cape of contentment, when in reality your desire is to look a little more like the filtered image you share on social media? Perhaps you've worn the cape of confidence, when you actually feel insecure because you constantly compare yourself to all the girls around you. It could be that you've covered yourself with the cape of happiness, even though deep down you feel unworthy because those who are supposed to love you most don't treat you as someone who holds great value.

Our culture does not honor Christ, and it pumps out messages promising you fulfillment in everything except God.[6] These messages are designed to make you dissatisfied and unhappy with who you are and what you don't have.

Messages like:
- You have to flaunt it to be noticed.
- You'll never be anything if you don't look like this.
- To be popular, you need to _____, and the more popular you are, the better.
- "Likes" matter.
- You need to be InstaFamous.
- The pretty girls are the thin ones.
- You need Botox.
- You need to wear this brand to be popular.
- You need, you need, you need.[7]

The world, society, and even some of your friends are pouring lies into you every day. Lies like, "You will never be enough." Every time you get on social media and view the flawless pictures of your friend or *what appears to be* that perfectly formed body and compare it to yourself, it leaves you feeling inadequate and unworthy. It is easy to buy into the idea that, "Everyone else is prettier than me," and, "I'm not perfect just the way God created me" when you are bombarded with an endless stream of carefully edited images. What we forget is that all we see on social media platforms is the "perfect" side of people. Your friends can take 300 selfies until they find just the right angle, and with a few quick fixes, they can make themselves look like someone you don't even recognize. Over time, falling into the comparison trap begins to negatively shape our thoughts and how we see ourselves.

In her book, *Get Out of Your Head*, Jennie Allen says, "The greatest spiritual battle of our generation is being fought between our ears."[8] I couldn't agree more! "How can something we can't see control so much of who we are, determine what we feel and what we do and what we say or don't, dictate how

26

we move or sleep, and inform what we want, what we hate and what we love," Allen writes.[9] We are often our own worst discouragers. Did you know that you have an average of 2,500 to 3,300 thoughts per hour, and your brain processes almost 70,000 thoughts per day?[10] What's even more mind-boggling is that 80 percent of our thoughts are negative![11]

Maybe you have experienced some of these awful toxic thoughts:

- "I'm ugly."
- "I'm fat."
- "I have no friends."
- "Everybody hates me."
- "I'll never get a boyfriend."
- "No one will love me. I'm unlovable."
- "I've sinned too much. God's not going to forgive me."

Cognitive distortions or negative thinking patterns can cause us to get stuck in our thoughts and hurt us emotionally. These patterns influence our beliefs and self-esteem. Psychologists conclude that negative thinking can lead to depression, chronic worry, anxiety, and obsessive-compulsive disorder.[12] Some people resort to harming themselves, like cutting or scratching, or using unhealthy ways of coping, such as illegal drugs, to hide the pain caused by constantly thinking negative thoughts.

Here are some of the most common negative thinking patterns:

1. **All or Nothing Thinking:** You see everything in black and white categories; there are no grey areas.
   - "I'll <u>always</u> be alone. I'll <u>never</u> have friends."

27

2. **Overgeneralization:** If you experience one negative event, you assume that it will continue to happen, leading to failure every time.
   - You fail one test, so you tell yourself, "Life is hopeless. I'll never graduate."

3. **Labeling:** When you make a general statement about yourself or someone else based on just one negative trait or experience and assume it represents the whole person.
   - Instead of saying, "I made a mistake," you tell yourself, "I'm stupid," "I'm a loser," and "I'm such an idiot."

4. **Jumping to Conclusions:**
   - Mind Reading—You assume that people are reacting negatively to you when there's no concrete evidence.
   - Fortune Telling—You randomly assume that things will go wrong.[13]

Taking Down the Enemy!

To take down the enemies of our mind, we have to learn to take our thoughts captive, challenge them, and s l o w l y begin to change them. We must use techniques that allow us to challenge our irrational thoughts and replace them with helpful, more positive ways of thinking. Using a thought diary is a way to discover your negative thinking patterns and gain a better understanding of how your thoughts cause your emotional reactions. Record the unfavorable thoughts that come into your mind and the emotions you experienced during that particular situation in a daily journal. Once you've identified the destructive messages occurring in your mind, you can use a simple technique, known as "S-O-S", to confront and challenge those negative thoughts.

S-top: Mentally tell yourself "Stop!" to give you the opportunity to address the thought and interrupt the cycle.

O-bserve: Observe what you are saying to yourself and how it is making you feel.

S-hift: Shift your cognitive, emotional, or behavioral reaction by using positive coping skills and techniques.[14]

Here's a few examples of how you can use the S-O-S technique:

- **Situation:** I'm seventeen, and I've never been asked out on a date.
- **Twisted Thought:** No one will ever want to be with me.
- **Positive Reframe:** I have lots of good qualities. God will help me find the right person one day.

- **Situation:** Your best friend, Sarah, sat by another friend at lunch.
- **Twisted Thought:** Sarah didn't come sit by me at lunch today. She must not like me anymore.
- **Positive Reframe:** Sarah has lots of friends. She probably just wanted to catch up with Lindsey today.

Remember, you identify the negative thought, and challenge it! Where did this thought come from? Am I looking at the whole picture? Would people I love and trust agree with these thoughts? Then, attempt to positively reframe it. Use a thought diary over several weeks, including each negative "twisted" thought, emotion, and a way to positively reframe to begin reshaping your thinking patterns. It takes practice, but you can do it! If you come to a point where you feel like your negative thinking patterns are affecting your daily life and ability to function, you may find it both helpful and necessary to meet with a Christian therapist. Mental health counselors can help you learn about what you're feeling, why you might be feeling it, and how to cope. Remember, the most well-rounded and successful people are those who use their resources to get help when they need it!

Seeking Spiritual Beauty

Another important method for shifting to a more positive thought pattern and self-image is to dwell on God's view of you. Our tendency is to focus exclusively on the outward appearance to give us a feeling of beauty and value, but those things won't make us feel complete. **You will imprison yourself if you define your value by the world's terms—the number of likes and shares on Instagram, your weight, your athletic skills, or the shape of your face.** You'll never be good enough for someone else's standards. You've got to believe God over the world. God already loves you. He knew you before you were born (Jeremiah 1:5). We must realize our worthiness is based upon being a child of God (1 John 3:1). You are a daughter of a King (2 Corinthians 6:18). You are a "chosen people, a royal priesthood, a holy nation, a people for *God's* own possession" (1 Peter 2:9). God knows how perfect and precious you are because you are His reflection. Psalms 147:3 tells us that He "heals the brokenhearted and binds up their wounds." It's Jesus' work on the cross that makes it possible for you to overcome the struggles you face. The fact that God was willing to send His Son to die for you shows you that you're worthy of everything.

There will always be a part of us that feels empty if our self-image is based entirely on the outward appearance. A Christian woman's self-worth should flow from the inner beauty she possesses. "Your adornment must not be merely the external—

braiding the hair, wearing gold jewelry, or putting on apparel; but it should be the hidden person of the heart, with the imperishable quality of a gentle and quiet spirit, which is precious in the sight of God" (1 Peter 3:3-4). Here are some attributes of a spiritually beautiful woman:

- Humble (Colossians 3:12)
- Patient and kind (1 Corinthians 13:4)
- Hard-working (Proverbs 31:13)
- Selfless (Philippians 2:4)
- Dignified (Proverbs 31:25)
- Loving (1 Peter 1:22)
- Servant (John 12:26)
- Modest (1 Timothy 2:9-10)
- God-fearing (Proverbs 31:30)

Don't ever forget where your beauty comes from. You are chosen, loved, adopted, redeemed, and forgiven (Ephesians 1). Oh, how I wish my grandmother would have taught me these beautiful truths instead! That is what gives you value. You are an expensive utensil made for great purposes! You will never feel complete or fully satisfied until you recognize your worth based on being created in His image (Genesis 1:27). You are a reflection of your Creator. Let that reflection radiate out from within. Stop hiding behind the capes! You are worth everything because the Creator made you and you are His workmanship. No one is perfect, so embrace the fact that you have flaws, and love the things that make you unique. You could lose every ounce of beauty you possess and every dollar you own but will never lose your value in being a child of God. Once you start recognizing the beauty you have from within, you'll find the healing and worth you've longed for.

It's Time for Reflection!

1. How has your personal identity been influenced by the culture around you?

2. In what ways have you let the world set your standard for beauty?

3. What qualities of a spiritually beautiful woman do you already possess?

4. What attributes of a Christian woman would you most like to obtain?

5. Do a character study on the Proverbs 31 woman by looking at her attributes and the lessons we can learn from her. Consider her character traits, relationships, roles, and responsibilities as you read this scripture.

6. Read the following verses and identify some of the character traits that made her beautiful (Hint: It wasn't her outward beauty!). You should be able to find at least one positive quality from each set of verses.

10-12: _____

13-16: _____

17-20: _____

21-24: _____

25-29: _____

30-31: _____

7. The worthy woman had numerous virtuous attributes that we each should aspire to obtain. Take some time to reflect on and jot down practical ways you can work towards developing these same qualities as a woman of God. For example, if you identified her as being a trustworthy individual, you might demonstrate it this week by keeping promises you make to your friends and family. See if you can find at least two qualities to focus on and pray about this week!

Chapter 4

Making Positive Entertainment Choices

♥ ♥ ♥ ♥ ♥ ♥ ♥ ♥ ♥ ♥ ♥ ♥ ♥ ♥ ♥ ♥ ♥ ♥

I f you've ever taught an early-elementary Bible class, you know kids that age will say the funniest, most outrageous, and innocent things. I'll never forget one particular student who, when asked about things we should not do as Christians, quickly responded, "You should never punch God!" I don't think I would have ever come up with that answer, but he sure was proud to have thought of it. Along with being very innocent, young children tend to also be very honest during Bible conversations. Once, when I was teaching second and third graders on the importance of being careful about what we listen to and watch, one of my students said, "My parents never care how much cussing is in movies." This little boy had very quickly picked up on the example his parents were setting in their entertainment choices.

Can you relate to this little boy? Perhaps it's not your parents but you who have no limits on what you allow to enter your heart through your entertainment choices. As a Christian, it is important to be aware of the content we consume and whether it aligns with our personal beliefs and values. There is nothing inherently wrong with enjoying mainstream entertainment. First Timothy 6:17 says that God "richly supplies us with all things to enjoy." But just because not everything is inherently bad doesn't mean there are no limits either. We live in an immoral world, and sometimes the good things God created can be used in sinful ways. As you begin this chapter, I want you to consider this: ***Are you really living differently from the world in your entertainment choices?***

Entertainment, including movies, television shows, and music, can influence our behaviors and beliefs. Media can provide role models, offer a new perspective on a wide range of topics, and serve as a source of inspiration. Many of us find entertainment as a way to escape, relax, and connect with friends and family. During your teen years, you are at a growth phase where you are forming your identity and learning how to navigate the world around you, which leaves you vulnerable to the influence of entertainment. For teens especially, music is extremely influential and is a significant part of your lives. It is important to be aware of the potential impact of media in your life and those around you.

Entertainment is a part of our everyday culture in America. According to the latest Common Sense Census Report, 77 percent of teens view online videos daily and spend an average of eight-and-a-half hours per day watching television, gaming, and using social media. That's a lot of time, isn't it?! It's important to be selective about the media we engage with and to consider the potential consequences.

Approved by Hollywood

In *Straddling the Fence,* a survey of teenagers found that 76 percent had viewed PG-13-rated movies and 68 percent had watched R-rated movies in the last six months.[1] If I asked you if it would affect your purity to view PG-13- or R-rated movies, what would your response be? Based on my own indifference during adolescence towards my media choices, my suspicion is most teenage girls would not view this as a "big deal." Let's look at some of the currently trending movies and TV series right now aimed at teens so we can explore their content. Here's a few:

- *Pretty Little Liars*
- *The Fallout*
- *Stranger Things*
- *Outer Banks*
- *Vampire Diaries*

Did you know all these TV series and movies have PG-13 or higher parental ratings? Many of these popular teen media choices contain harmful messages and ideas. For example, *The Fallout* has thirty-two uses of sexually inappropriate expressions and offensive language, seventeen uses of moderate profanity, and repeated uses of irreverence towards deity.[2] The cast of the latest *Pretty Little Liars: Original Sin* series has several LGBT characters and has strong sexual elements, frequent cursing, and underage drinking and smoking.[3] *Outer Banks* is described as an "edgy guilty pleasure," with recurrent use of language that is offensive and disrespectful towards God.[4] The Motion Picture Association's guidelines for PG-13 ratings allow "more than brief nudity," the use of drugs, and the inclusion of one of the stronger "sexually-derived words," like an expletive.[5] R-rated movies may have adult themes and values that don't align with Christian values, such as "hard language, intense or persistent violence, sexually-oriented nudity, drug abuse or other elements, so that parents are counseled to take this rating very seriously."[6] *What kind of things are we allowing to infiltrate our minds when we view these types of media, even if our parents permit it?*

The Third Commandment:

A common misconception among Christians is that we can filter out all the negative input that comes into our minds from media. But, what goes in will eventually come out. We slowly become desensitized to sin. One area where Christian teens have become indifferent is in showing disrespect for God's name. It's absolutely everywhere! But is it really a big deal to watch TV or listen to music that disrespects the Lord? Let's see what the Bible has to say about how God's name is to be used. We find this first mentioned in the writing of the Ten Commandments. In Exodus 20:7, it states, "You shall not take the name of the Lord your

God in vain, for the Lord will not leave him unpunished who takes His name in vain." How did "watch your mouth" make the top ten? Does it really matter to God? You better believe it does! It was so important to our Lord that we honor and respect His name that He chose this command as one of only ten under the Mosaic Law. So, what exactly is forbidden by the third commandment? The word *vain* can mean "empty," "nothing," or "worthless."[7] We are prohibited from using the Lord's name in ways that are meaningless, evil, or for inappropriate reasons.

We've already learned that breaking the third commandment is considered a significant sin, but what makes it so serious? God's name is holy, and it is to be respected. God told the Israelites, "Moreover, the one who blasphemes the name of the Lord must be put to death; all the congregation shall certainly stone him. The stranger as well as the native, when he blasphemes the Name, shall be put to death" (Leviticus 24:16). Under the Law of Moses, the consequence was severe for those who blasphemed the name of the Lord. Webster defines blaspheming as "the act of insulting or showing contempt or lack of reverence for God."[8] Of course, these instances were under the Old Law, but do you think God's still just as concerned about us honoring and respecting His name now? Based on what I read in His Word, I would say emphatically, yes! God's character has not changed. Malachi 3:6 tells us, "For I, the Lord, do not change." It's just as important today as it was so many years ago, to honor and respect His name.

What's Your Price?

Constantly exposing yourself to bad entertainment choices not only violates the third commandment but also leads to other negative outcomes. As a teenager it is important for you to be discerning about the values and messages being presented through music, TV, and movies. Entertainment can have a negative effect on your spiritual growth and development if it presents unhealthy or unrealistic messages and values. For example, pop culture and Hollywood often romanticize sex. A survey of the top grossing movies released from 1950 to 2006 found that more than 84 percent contained sexual content, and this was not limited to R-rated films. In fact, 68 percent of G-rated movies, 82 percent of PG-rated movies, 85 percent of PG-13-rated movies, and 88 percent of R-rated movies all referenced sexual situations.[9] Imagine the impact it is going to have on your purity if you're spending up to eight hours a day viewing media that glamorizes sex and contains explicit nudity. The negative messages thrown at us will begin to normalize sin and make us less sensitive to these behaviors.

It can also give a distorted view of what God identifies as acceptable. The National Library of Medicine conducted a study and found that "sexually explicit media exposure in early adolescence was strongly related to three risky sexual behaviors—early sexual debut, unsafe sex, and sexual partners—in late adolescence, and this relationship was very close to causal."[10] This is just one example of how what you allow to enter your mind can influence your decisions and behaviors in negative ways.

A major concern with media consumption is the potential for it to dull our sensitivity to sinful activities and values. If you really believe your entertainment choices do not influence your thoughts and beliefs, why is advertising a $285.21 billion dollar industry?[11] The United States spends more on advertising than any other country in the world. Why? Because advertising has an impact on making behaviors and values seem normal. Our world is working as hard and as fast as it possibly can to make sin seem ordinary. We tend to discredit the effect that desensitization has on us. Here's a personal example. When I was teenager, not one person I knew questioned their gender, but now that gender identity has penetrated every media platform we consume, it's become a question for many teens. It's the same reason that the idea of incest would disgust you (*and seem far worse in your mind*) than that idea of being homosexual. You've become less sensitive to it because it's been normalized by our society.

As you consider your media engagement, take a minute to do some personal reflection as you think about the following questions. Would your worldly friends think you are any different from them based on what you listen to, look at on your phone, or watch on TV? Do your Instagram reels, YouTube shorts, and TikTok feeds contain different content from your non-Christian friends, or do you look so much like the world they cannot tell the difference?

We are advised in 1 John 2:15-16, "Do not love the world nor the things in the world. If anyone loves the world, the love of the Father is not in him. For all that is in the world, the lust of the flesh and the lust of the eyes and the boastful pride of life, is not from the Father, but is from the world." The Bible tells us to "set your mind on things above, not on things that are on Earth" (Colossians 3:2). Instead of following the world's standards for media, we should seek to find wholesome entertainment that aligns with the written words in Philippians 4:8: "Finally, brothers and sisters, whatever is true, whatever is honorable, whatever is right, whatever is pure, whatever is lovely, whatever is commendable, if there is any excellence and if anything worthy of praise, think about these things."

Is it hard to find good, clean entertainment? Yes, absolutely! However, just because it's difficult to locate family-friendly content does not give us the freedom to take on the world's standards. **God's laws are not lessened because American culture makes it challenging to find wholesome entertainment**

for Christians to engage in. We've all heard Christians compromise on entertainment, justifying it with the argument that they couldn't watch anything if they turned off the TV every time they heard the Lord's name disrespected. Remember, God is more concerned with our holiness than our happiness. It may not be easy to do, but it can be done.

What Should We Do?

Establishing rules and boundaries for the media content you consume will help you in maintaining your purity with Christ. When I was in high school, an elder in the church told me his family set a limit of three profanities for any entertainment viewing before turning it off. This was the best advice I could have been given as a teen. Prior to this, I hadn't set firm boundaries for myself, nor had my parents. When I began setting limits, it really helped me become more mindful of the things I was allowing to enter my heart. I adjusted my limits slightly when my kids suggested turning the channel anytime they heard the Lord's name used inappropriately. How could I argue with that? But, I'm not here to dictate *how* you set your standard; instead, I encourage you to establish your own. If you don't, you'll find yourself allowing more to enter into your heart than you initially intended.

Here are some general rules that can help you maintain purity in your entertainment choices:

- Be proactive in determining the content you feel comfortable viewing and set boundaries for what you watch or listen to.

- Use online filtering services that give you the ability to take profanity, nudity, sexual situations, and graphic violence out of the media you view.

❇ Utilize the "Restricted Mode" on video sharing apps. This optional setting will filter out the majority of the "mature content" and sexually inappropriate material.

❇ Avoid media content that is sexually explicit or otherwise offensive. You don't want it to ruin your mind.

❇ Set boundaries around the location where you will view entertainment. I strongly encourage you to keep your media viewing out of your bedroom. We tend to loosen our standards in privacy. Keep your devices in the main areas of the home where you have a little more accountability.

❇ Consider talking to a mature Christian you trust about your struggles with entertainment choices and seek their advice on how to set your standards.

As we conclude our discussion on entertainment, a meaningful quote comes to mind, "Ships don't sink because of the water around them, ships sink because of the water that gets in them." While we may not have control of everything that happens around us, we do have power over what enters our minds and shapes us spiritually. The content we consume will positively influence or negatively impact our hearts. When we watch media that promotes sin, it can weigh us down and draw us away from our faith. Don't let the world dictate your entertainment standards. Romans 12:2 encourages us, "And do not be conformed to this world, but be transformed by the renewing of your mind, so that you may prove what the will of God is, that which is good and acceptable and perfect." We cannot live a holy and acceptable life when our entertainment choices contradict God's nature. Establish firm boundaries for your media choices and stick to them. By reintroducing purity into our entertainment decisions, we can live in a way that is set apart from the world and honors God through our media consumption.

It's Time for Reflection!

1. On a scale from 1-10 (1: "I don't pay any attention to my media choices" to 10: "I have strict limits set in place on entertainment, and I follow them well"), how well do you do in selecting clean, uplifting entertainment?

2. What kind of rules do you have in place already to help you keep purity in the area of entertainment?

3. In what areas do you need to improve?

4. Write out some rules that you can implement to better maintain your purity around entertainment. Begin working on putting these boundaries into place this week. Take a few minutes each night over the next two weeks to monitor your progress. You can do this! I bet you'll be happily surprised about your improvement when you start implementing these changes.

Chapter 5

Embracing Modest Attire

✔ ✔ ✔ ✔ ✔ ✔ ✔ ✔ ✔ ✔ ✔ ✔ ✔ ✔ ✔ ✔ ✔

I spent my teenage years in a small military town located just twenty minutes from the nearest beach. As you can imagine, the clothing standards lessen with every mile closer you live to a beach. On top of that, the south Georgia heat index felt like 120 degrees in mid-summer, so less was best as it related to attire. I still remember how I begged my Mom as an early teen for this two-piece, island-floral bikini top and swim shorts *(the shorts made it more modest, of course)* until she caved and let me get it. I also recall the time my Sunday morning Bible teacher called me out for wearing a green corduroy skirt that was so short it clearly had no business being in my repertoire of clothes. It wasn't until I went to Faulkner University that my thoughts on modesty changed. More on how that all transpired later.

Modesty is defined as "behaving, dressing, or speaking in a way that is considered proper or decorous; decent; not-pretentious."[1] Modesty encompasses *far more* than just our attire, as discussed in other chapters of this book. However, this chapter is focusing on the aspect of purity that has the potential to revolutionize the church—what we wear. But, wow, can this topic spark debate among teen girls and their Christian mamas!

From my experience, it seems that many women are not sure what biblical modesty is because it is a rarely discussed subject. Maybe we're concerned with the backlash if we confront Christians with a need to make drastic changes, or perhaps we don't even know whether the Bible defines modest dress. We know from verses like 1 Corinthians 6:20 that we "have been bought for a price" and we should "glorify God in your body." As a teen, you should be standing out as an example of what modesty looks like to the world around you. First Timothy 4:12 says, "Let no one look down on your youthfulness, but rather in speech, conduct, love, faith, and purity, show yourself an example of those who believe." As Christian women, we should be dressing in a way that shows we are worthy of honor and respect. My goal in writing this chapter is to *hopefully* introduce a fresh perspective for us to consider on modesty. Please don't rip out the pages and use them as lighter fuel just yet! Stick with me and try to keep an open mind.

Modest dress appears to be relatively effortless for many Christian teens as it relates to "church attire." However, when it comes to extracurricular activities like sports, hanging with friends, formal events, or when you're within fifty feet of a body of water, you tend to blend in with the world! We've all seen it—girls dressed in T-shirts longer than their shorts, girls wearing sports attire that leaves nothing to the imagination, or even Christian moms who post pictures of their beautiful daughters on social media wearing bikinis. Most Christians are completely desensitized to it. Christians have allowed society to set our standard for modest dress. **We've allowed culture, not God, to**

define modesty. We can read in 1 Peter 3:3-4 that our personal fulfillment and beauty should come from our inward being not our outside appearance. However, too many Christians take an apathetic approach to modesty, and when they see other Christians doing the same, they think, "Well, they wear it, so why can't I?" *What if Noah would have taken that approach to godly living?* **<u>You</u>** can change church culture, girls! Don't let your parents, your Bible class teachers, and certainly not the world set your standard for modesty. Turn *only* to God's Word. If we're going to flip the world upside down for Jesus, this is an area where we *MUST* take a stand.

In talking to many teenage girls about what purity involves, they have all agreed that modesty is the toughest part for them. I totally agree! When I was a teen, I felt like I had a relatively good understanding of the type of young woman God wanted me to be…except in the area of modesty. I don't remember many women giving me practical strategies on how to dress modestly, so I didn't have the best barometer. On top of that, as I began to learn more, I felt like modesty meant I had to shop in the boys' department for shorts. The clothes made me feel ugly, and I obviously stood out. It was so hard!

As I reflect on my own personal journey with modesty, I've wondered, "If my faithful Christian parents allowed me to wear it, how can these clothes be immodest?" Y'all, I truly had the most spiritual mom ever. I love her and the godly example she set for me with every fiber of my being! And yet, I'm still perplexed at times when I think back to some of the clothing I was permitted to wear as a teen. Why would my mom, who truly loved God and wanted nothing more than for us to follow in the footsteps of Jesus, allow me to wear some of the things I did? Here's where I think it stems from—I want you to visualize that six-month-old baby picture of you with those big innocent eyes and sweet chubby cheeks. You remember, the one where you could've won the Gerber Baby Contest? Got that mental picture going yet? Okay. I truly believe your mom and dad still see you as that sweet little Gerber baby. Their image of you is still a cute and innocent child. What your parents see when they look at you is NOT how the guys walking down the hallways at school, your gym partners, or your male friends at the beach see you! Our parents, or all our family, for that matter, view us through a completely different lens than most guys do.

Would You Visit the Jail Dressed Like That?

In *Seeking Spiritual Beauty*, the author references a man who volunteered with the jail ministry and noticed a sign in the waiting room about the requirements for visiting inmates at the jail.[2] The sign was unique, as it was posted multiple times, unlike all the other signs. If you're like me, you probably assume a sign posted repeatedly would say to not wear jewelry, and not bring in guns, tobacco, or illegal substances. No doubt signs about contraband are posted in jails, however, the sign displayed multiple times was all about dress.[3] This concept piqued my curiosity, so I decided to pull up the dress code requirements for visitation at correctional facilities across the state of Georgia where I live, and here is what it says:

> What is the dress code for visitation? Visitors are required to wear appropriate attire. Shoes are required at all times for visitors, including children if they are able to walk or stand. Male visitors will be required to wear shirts and full-length trousers. Females may wear trousers, or if a female visitor wears a dress, skirt, or other similar garment, it may NOT be more than two (2) inches above the knees. Furthermore, all female vis-

itors must wear foundation-type garments such as bras, panties, and slip. Inappropriate clothing shall include, but not be limited to:

- Dresses or tops with thin straps which expose shoulders or chest area in any manner;
- tube tops or halters of any type;
- any type of clothing which reveals the stomach or midriff area;
- any type of clothing that is made of sheer or transparent material;
- shorts of any kind or any kind of slacks that are above the knee (twelve (12) years old and under may wear shorts);
- Male visitors are not permitted to wear tank tops or short tops of any kind, nor see-through tops made of net or mesh webbing. Shorts are not permitted (children twelve (12) years old and under may wear shorts).
- Any other type of clothing that is suggestive or revealing in any way shall be prohibited.[4]

Why are the visitation requirements to penitentiaries so strict? Are you shocked by any of these? Notice that the dress code for these facilities is not written by your preacher, your grandma, or your old-school Bible class teacher. This is written by the State Board of Corrections, which is made up of members from each prison district and five individuals selected by the governor. This Board understands that how you and I dress could negatively affect the inmates under their supervision. These high-governing officials are aware of the problems that inappropriate attire can create and work hard to prevent avoidable issues. They also understand the differences in the way male and female brains process information. Guys often get aroused through what they see, while girls tend to feel more based on emotions. Here's the bottom line: guys are attracted to you differently than you are to them! These policy writers understand that when inmates get visually stimulated by the way a woman dresses, it could lead to targeting of other inmates and violence towards the administration or the visitors. I know we don't live in a penitentiary, but it should be eye-opening to see there are consequences to our dress. So, girls, the correctional facilities have laid out a good rule of thumb for you to consider when determining how you should dress from an objective, and even worldly, perspective. This is not your Christian-school or your Bible-camp dress code!

How We're Wired: Male vs. Female Brain

During my teenage years, I really didn't understand just how differently the male and female brains worked, so it caused me confusion and frustration when it came to modesty. And, honestly, it's unlikely many teenagers do. This is why God gave us parents and older Christians to guide us. I was one of those girls who would argue until I was blue in the face that what you wear should fit the occasion. I wouldn't wear mini skirts to church, but I didn't have a problem wearing much less when I was participating in other activities. I clearly remember saying things in college like, "You wouldn't wear a complete suit and tie to run in, so why would you wear full clothing (*shorts and a T-shirt*) swimming?" It made sense in my mind. Let me share what changed things for me.

In college, some of my close guy friends openly expressed how difficult it was to think pure thoughts when girls wore tight, revealing clothing, no matter where they were. I could argue with a lot of things, but I couldn't argue with that! But, you don't have to take my friends' word for it. Science has long revealed that males are generally more interested in and have a stronger reaction to visual, sexually-stimulating things compared to females. In neuroscience studies, using brain scans, they found that in guys, certain parts of the brain (like the amygdala and hypothalamus) light up more than in girls when they look at the sexual stuff.[5] This helps explain why there is a significantly higher percentage of males (87.6%) reporting the use of porn compared to females (40.9%).[6] God created a difference between males and females in the way that the brain processes information.

In 1 Corinthians 8:9-13, God reminds us not to be a stumbling block to others. If we can prevent our Christian brothers—whose brains are wired differently and may not have learned how to bounce their eyes—from stumbling into sin, then that's something we should do![7] We've all heard, and maybe even thought, "It's not my fault if someone else looks and lusts!" That's not entirely true. Think about Mark 9:42, which says, "Whoever causes one of these little ones who believe in Me to sin, it is better for him if a heavy millstone is hung around his neck and he is thrown into the sea." I'm not saying guys aren't responsible too! I know both guys and girls play a part, but this book is written for girls. That's why I'm highlighting the changes we can make. We must understand that part of our responsibility with modesty is in our relationship to our brothers in Christ. You probably have a close guy friend you love and want to help support in honoring the Lord with his thoughts and actions. Let your love for your brothers in Christ motivate you to dress in a way that glorifies God and helps them in their walk with Christ.

From a Biblical Perspective

Did you know that the Bible actually provides examples of modesty for us? I know, I was surprised by this, too, when I first started digging into this subject! Let's jump in by going all the way back to when humanity first disobeyed God and brought sin and death into the world. In Genesis 3, Eve is deceived by the serpent and eats the forbidden fruit, and Adam soon follows suit. Immediately afterwards, "the eyes of both of them were opened, and they knew that they were naked; and they sewed fig leaves together and made themselves waist coverings." Waist coverings are commonly referred to as loincloths. A loincloth is defined as "a type of clothing that is draped around the hips and groin. It is generally made in one piece but sometimes it is kept in place by a belt."[8] In cultures that did not approve of showing private body parts, it was worn as an undergarment or swimsuit. If you're familiar with a loincloth, you know it provides minimal coverage to the private areas of the body. Was that a sufficient covering for Adam and Eve? No, the couple hid after making coverings for themselves when they heard God walking around in the garden because they were afraid when they realized they were still naked (Genesis 3:8-10).

If you read further in chapter 3, you'll see what God did to fix the situation. In Genesis 3:21, it says, "And the Lord God made garments of skin for Adam and his wife, and clothed them." The Hebrew word used for "garments" in this verse is *Kethoneth,* which means a tunic or covering.[9] Webster's Dictionary defines a tunic as "a simple slip-on garment made with or without sleeves and usually knee-length or longer."[10] It's interesting that God assisted the first husband and wife, and the only two people on Earth, in dressing modestly! *Do you believe that God was aware of the potential for immodest dress to become a more common issue as the population grew and even intended for their clothing choices to serve as an example for future generations to follow?[11]*

Let's shift our focus to the book of Exodus. In Exodus 28, we learn about the requirements for Aaron and his sons when they entered the tabernacle or ministered in the Holy Place.

40 "For Aaron's sons you shall also make tunics; you shall also make sashes for them, and you shall make caps for them, for glory and for beauty. 41 Then you shall put them on Aaron your brother and on his sons with him; and you shall anoint them and ordain them and consecrate them, so that they may serve Me as priests. 42 You shall make for them linen undergarments to cover their bare flesh; they shall reach from the waist even to the thighs. 43 And they shall be on Aaron and on his sons when they enter the tent of meeting, or when they approach the altar to minister in the Holy Place, so that they do not incur guilt and die. It shall be a statute forever to him and to his descendants after him."

We can see in verse 42 that they were to wear tunics, sashes, caps, and linen undergarments that covered their bare flesh from the waist to the thighs. Now, most of you are probably like me and when you think of the word "thigh," you're only thinking mid-thigh *(the "my shorts only have to reach the end of my finger-tips" rule to be in line with the thigh)*. But, that is not an accurate definition of the thigh. If you look up the definition, the thigh is actually the part of the leg that extends from the top of the hip to the knee.[12] If God was concerned with the modesty of His chosen people all those years ago, do you think He's still concerned about it today? Although we are not priests entering the holy of holies, as Christians, we are a "chosen people, a royal priesthood, a holy nation, a people for God's own possession" (1 Peter 2:9). While I'm not suggesting that this is a hard-and-fast rule for us to follow today, this biblical passage provides us a starting point—a glimpse of what God found acceptable under the Old Law.

Guiding Principles:

As Christians, we should be dressing in a way that demonstrates reverence and honor towards God. We have let the world slip in and blind us to truth in the area of modest apparel for too long. We've got to rethink our ideas. It's time to start asking ourselves, "Am I glorifying God in what I wear?" We've discussed what the Bible says, now, let's explore how these principles guide two areas where people often tend to bend the rules of modest dressing. Let's start with our swim attire. In 1946, French designer Louis Reard released the first two-piece bikini, aiming to reveal a new side of women by exposing the belly button.[13] Facing resistance, no model wanted to wear such a scandalous outfit. In 1957, *Modern Girl Magazine* said, "The bikini was hardly necessary to waste words on, because no girl with tact or decency would ever wear such a thing."[14] Reard eventually chose a stripper to model the swimsuit. Wow, have we come a long way in what we identify as acceptable to God! Recently, in a Bible study, a young man shared, "I used to stop and look when I saw a girl in a bikini on social media. Now, I try to scroll past it."

Modest dress is not situational; males cannot turn off the sexually-stimulating part of their brains just because you've entered a body of water. Furthermore, if a bikini is modest, what qualifies as immodest? Girls, do you realize that most bras and underwear contain more fabric than a bikini? Can you imagine going to the movies or mall with your guy friends in just that? You'd be horrified—and rightly so! Let's not get stuck on bikinis, though. There are many other swimsuits that are just as immodest. Here's a good principle to follow: if your swim attire doesn't set you apart from your non-Christian friends, there is an issue. Society has desensitized us to what's considered appropriate swimwear! Cute alternatives like board shorts and rashguards exist. But, honestly, even if they didn't,

God wants your holiness over you fitting in.

When discussing modest clothing, our focus tends to be solely on swimwear, but immodesty extends well beyond bikinis. We should glorify God whether we're at school, the pool, or on the ball field. I've observed a significant shift in the realm of sports. Athletic attire for sporting events—at both Christian and public schools—has become increasingly less modest. In many pictures posted by schools on social media, one could not differentiate between a "Christian" or "public" school because the attire looks virtually identical! As a general rule, if your audience can't see that you have shorts on because your shirt covers them, reconsider wearing that uniform. Spandex alone should not be considered shorts. Spandex is tight and visually outlines every part of your body. Wearing clothing like that makes it challenging to glorify God.

Many girls use the excuse, "But the school requires me to wear this." Well, how do school administrations or recreational leagues respond when someone from a different faith wants to adjust their clothing due to religious reasons? They let them change their attire! There was a basketball player of the Muslim faith playing on the opposing team of my child, and she wore modest clothes and a hijab head covering throughout the entire basketball game without any qualms from the league. *We must take a stand if we want a change.* Tell your school that it violates your faith to wear a uniform that is tight or short. If they won't allow you to wear something different, reach out to your parents, a minister, an elder, or another spiritual mentor in your church. You may even have to be willing to quit the team because you are worthy—and this is a worthy cause that we need to be prepared to fight for.

As you evaluate your wardrobe, consider these guiding principles:

❀ When selecting your outfit, ask these questions:
  • Can I bring honor to God in this outfit?
  • Will wearing it make it more difficult for my Christian brothers to maintain pure thoughts?

❀ For cleavage and midriff: Keep it covered.

❀ Regarding shorts and skirts: I personally opt for lengths closer to my knee. I'm not suggesting you need to mirror my style. I understand there is room for variation. But, let me encourage you to establish a personal standard and stay committed to it.

❀ Avoid seeking advice from worldly sources! Talk with mature women in your church to get sound, biblical guidance on modest apparel. Their wisdom can assist you in determining appropriate clothing choices.

Teenage years are tough, and the temptation to fit in is great. My heart goes out to you girls. Having conversations with teen girls, I know it is not easy to take a stand, especially when it means you have to look different. But we cannot straddle the fence! "Satan owns the fence," says gospel preacher Eric Garner. Don't have the "let's see how close I can get to sin without sinning" mentality. It's not worth it. God has called us to a life of holiness (1 Peter 1:16), and modesty falls into that category. Dressing in ways that are not in accordance with God's teaching can lead to promiscuous and unwanted attention, even if that wasn't your initial intention. Girls who prioritize spiritual beauty will dress in a way that brings honor, not lustful glances. If we're going to turn the world upside down for Christ, it starts with you and me. You and I will have to be the visual representation of what modest dress looks like for the world around us.

It's Time for Reflection!

1. This week take a good, honest, long look in the mirror. It's time to re-evaluate your wardrobe. Based on what you've read, would you identify your attire as modest?

2. Are you able to bring glory to God in the way you currently dress? If not, would you consider purchasing alternative outfits that still make you feel beautiful but will also bring glory and honor to God?

3. Write down a few things you need to change about your wardrobe. Pray this week that God will help you have a heart for dressing modestly and the strength and courage to stand for Him in this area.

Chapter 6

Navigating Technology in the Digital Age

✔ ✔ ✔ ✔ ✔ ✔ ✔ ✔ ✔ ✔ ✔ ✔ ✔ ✔ ✔ ✔

I didn't get my first phone until I was eighteen and headed off to college six hours from home. I even had to share it with my older brother (Ugh! Not fair). We had a few disagreements (to put it mildly) over whose turn it was to use the phone, an old Nokia 3310 with T-9 texting. Have y'all even heard of T-9 technology? To text, you had to press a key multiple times to type out a single letter, and if you were lucky, T-9 would suggest the right word for you. We became experts at pressing tiny buttons with our thumbs. Fast forward ten years, and smartphones were widely popular. I fell in love with the Apple iPhone and was using it every day for work, family life, and viewing social media. Before long, it became very hard to disconnect. I even began to struggle to resist the urge to check notifications and scroll Facebook while driving or at every single stop light. I felt myself becoming increasingly anxious and uncomfortably attached to my device. Do you ever get any of these feelings when you're on your phone?

Glorifying God with My Smartphone Use

The latest statistics from the Pew Research Center indicate that 95 percent of teens have access to smartphones. Additionally, 97 percent of teens use the internet daily.[1] The Common Sense Census survey reports that teens spend an average of nine hours per day on media *not including* time spent at school or on homework.[2] Wow, that's a lot of time! But, it's not just teens who are attached to their phones. On average, Americans look at their phones 344 times per day, which is about once every four minutes, and 47 percent consider themselves "addicted" to their phones. A shocking 35 percent use their phone while driving, and 43 percent will look at their phone while on a date. Sadly, 45 percent identify their phone as their *most valuable possession.*[3]

There's no doubt that phones have become integrated into everything we do, but how is the rise in technology use affecting us? A recent study of Canadian teens and young adults, ages thirteen to twenty-one, completed by the Universities of Western Ontario and Regina, found that high smartphone use—two hours or more a day—made it almost twice as likely that they would show signs of anxiety. In addition, high smartphone use was connected with almost three times higher risk of negative self-evaluation, mental health, and suicide thoughts.[4] China reports having over 20 million internet-addicted teens and has implemented strict tech regulations to help control the problem.[5] Technology addiction has become so prevalent in South Korea, they have opened 400 tech-rehabilitation facilities, and every student, teacher, and parent has been given a handbook alerting them to the potential dangers of screens and technology.[6]

 **Grab your phone! Let's do a screen-time check. How many hours a day are you using your device for personal entertainment? What are your most used apps? How many times do you pick up your phone a day? Is your current usage similar to teens across the United States?**

The Brain & Technology

To understand how technology impacts purity, you need to have a basic understanding of the brain. I know it might seem a little odd to talk about the brain in a book about purity, but I hope it'll help you understand the science behind why you feel and behave the way you do. Jesus says the eyes are the window to the soul—what you do with your eyes matters. I like the simple analogy of the brain being like a two-story house.[7] If you're thinking about your brain like a house, the bottom floor, or the downstairs brain, is part of the limbic system. This is responsible for our basic functions and responses, like breathing, heart rate, and emotions—it's more of the feelings brain.[8] The upstairs brain houses a more complex part of the brain called the prefrontal cortex. This part of your brain is responsible for many things, like making good decisions, impulse control, and evaluating risks.[9] So how are these fancy parts of your brain affected by your phone?

Your Developing Brain: The Prefrontal Cortex

The prefrontal cortex is one area of your brain that changes the most dramatically between the ages of ten and nineteen years old. The prefrontal cortex undergoes significant brain development during your teen years and doesn't reach full maturity until your mid-twenties.[10] So, as a teen, you might have a harder time resisting the addictive power of technology because your brain isn't fully ready to handle it yet.

Here are a few ways you could be impacted by excessive tech usage:
- Increased impulsive behaviors leading to Attention Deficit Hyperactivity Disorder (ADHD)
- Delayed sleep onset, sleep disturbances, and poor sleep quality[11]
- Poor language development
- Poor decision making and difficulty regulating emotions
- Social isolation[12]

How is My Screen Time Affecting Me?
- I can't stop watching media that contains sexual content.
- I'm afraid I'll miss out on something if I don't always stay connected on social media.
- I feel like I'm the only one at church who has no friends.
- I'm often disconnected from my friends when I'm with them because I'm scrolling TikTok or Instagram.
- I fall sleep about 12:30am after watching countless hours of YouTube, wake up numerous times a night when my friends text, and am exhausted when I get up.
- I feel very anxious a lot of the time.
- I constantly feel the urge to check notifications and social media even during Bible class and worship.

- I routinely make poor choices even though I don't want to.
- I see how happy everyone else is on social media and I feel so sad and alone.

Why Am I Addicted? The Dopamine Response!

Dopamine is often referred to as a pleasure chemical because it gives you feelings of enjoyment and satisfaction as part of the brain's reward system. Shopping with friends, working out, eating something you like, and even sex can all trigger a dopamine release. Dopamine is also released with every Snapchat notification, text message "ding," and Instagram "like" we receive. When our body does something rewarding, our brain releases dopamine, which says, "Do it again!" Our brains are wired for finding immediate reward, and technology gives us something new all the time. This can make us want to keep using technology because it feels good to get something new.[13]

Let's talk about this in a way most teen girls can understand—your love for posting on social media platforms. A Harvard University study found that self-disclosure on social media platforms can activate the areas of the brain associated with pleasure and reward.[14] This means that the act of sharing personal information can be rewarding and even addictive, similar to how someone might feel after taking a drug or consuming alcohol. So, for example, if you post a picture of yourself on social media and receive a lot of likes and positive comments, your brain might feel a rush of pleasure or satisfaction. This can encourage you to keep posting and sharing more about yourself to receive that positive feedback. This is because our brain reward centers are most active when we talk about ourselves. Can you see how this could become addictive behavior that could start to influence who you are and what you do, or worse, what you will feel tempted to share next?

Connected?

With the rise of social media, we are more connected than ever before, kind of. There are currently over 4.74 billion social media users worldwide. Despite the fact that over 75 percent of the world's population aged thirteen and older uses social media, we have to ask ourselves, does this usage genuinely make us happier?[15] For instance, teenage girls make up a significant portion of social media users, with 73 percent of those aged fifteen to seventeen using Instagram, the most popular social networking platform within this age group.[16] On average, girls between sixteen and twenty-four years old spend an average of three hours and ten minutes every day on social media. It's intriguing that more than half the users mention staying connected with friends and family as the main reason for using the internet.[17] As a species that is inherently designed for social connection, these statistics should be a wonderful thing and *ideally,* we should be walking around with smiles on our faces.[18]

"We are the loneliest society in human history."[19]
~ Johann Hari
(Best-selling author and leader on mental health)

Generation Z (those born since 1997) is the loneliest generation on record, with higher rates of isolation and being cut from social contact with others than both millennials and members of Generation X.[20] Being alone and feeling lonely have caused more mental health problems. A 2023 report from the Center for Disease Control looked at data from 2011 to 2021 and discovered that sixty percent of girls in school had continuous feelings of sadness or hopelessness during the past year.[21] High social media usage has been linked to increased feelings of loneliness in teens as compared to those with lower social media use.[22] In addition, among girls ten to fourteen, self-harm rates are up 189 percent since 2010.[23]

How is my tech usage contributing to my own feelings of loneliness? Am I missing out on important conversations with my friends because I'm too connected to my device? Is it distracting me from my relationship with God? Is it time to disconnect?

The Illusion of Connection

How often have you created the illusion of happiness and connection to your friends on social media when in actuality you were constantly comparing every aspect of your life to theirs? It's emotionally draining and ultimately leaves us unfulfilled. Why is this? "Electronic connection does not seem to satisfy the deep-seated need for true human contact. What in fact seems to have been spawned has been the illusion of social connection," says tech addiction expert Dr. Nicholas Kardaras.[24] Face-to-face interactions are an important part of building healthy relationships. Take something as simple as eye contact—we communicate numerous emotions through this form of non-verbal communication. Research has shown that eye contact triggers the limbic mirror system, meaning that when you share eye contact with someone, the neurons firing in your brain will also fire in theirs. This helps you share emotional states, increases empathy between individuals, and can help you bond with them.[25] *You cannot get this interacting with your device!*

So, what's the cure for a tech addiction? "The opposite of addiction isn't sobriety. The opposite of addiction is connection."[26] Not only is social connection a fundamental aspect of being human, but it is also a key ingredient to our general happiness and overall well-being. If you have a true crisis in your life, it won't be your Instagram followers or TikTok subscribers who provide comfort or help turn your life around. Your real-life, in-person friends, the ones you can touch and see, are the people who will have strong, committed relationships with you. There is a physiological aspect of friendship that your online friends can never replace. We are reminded in Hebrews 10:24-25 that to "encourage one another in love and good deeds," we must spend time together. If you don't learn how to develop in-person friendships, you will struggle to get through the difficult challenges life presents to you. Your social media friendships will simply not be enough. Is it time for you to put down the device so you can begin developing the relationships you need to sustain your walk with Christ?

How To Determine If You Might Have a Screen Problem

Tech addiction and mental health expert Dr. Nicholas Kardaras developed the following list of questions to help confirm a screen or tech addiction problem:

- Are you staying up later and later to stay on the computer?
- Do you get fidgety, anxious, and/or angry if you don't have your device?
- Is your tech usage negatively impacting your schoolwork, family life, or other activities or interests?
- Do you have a difficult time getting virtual imagery out of your head?

- Do you dream of virtual imagery?
- Do you hide your screen usage or device from your parents?
- Do you seem to have a more difficult time regulating your emotions?
- Do you feel apathetic or bored more easily?
- Do you feel perpetually tired yet also wired ("wired and tired")?
- Do your teachers complain that you're falling asleep in school?[27]

Dr. Kardaras reports that any one or combination of symptoms or behaviors from the above list could be a red flag for screen or tech addiction.

Note: This list originally found in the book Glow Kids has been adapted to fit teens.

If you feel like your current level of technology has become a problem in your life, reach out to a mental health professional who specializes in technology addictions. They can help you establish healthy and reasonable boundaries. If you don't have access to a counselor, reach out to your Bible class teacher, minister, or another trusted adult in your church for advice.

Media Guidelines: What's Recommended?

Although there are moments when I wish I could gather all the devices in the world and toss them off Mount Everest, banning screen use is not the solution. Research studies report that technology can be extremely beneficial to teenagers when used in the right capacity and with appropriate boundaries in place. So how do we effectively use tech for entertainment and relationship-building without getting trapped in addiction or compromising our values and well-being to these devices? Opinions differ on what a reasonable amount of media consumption is for teenagers. The American Academy of Child and Adolescent Psychiatry (AACAP) recommends limiting screen time by turning off devices during meals and outings, using parental controls, and removing screens from bedrooms before bedtime.[28] The Canadian Society for Exercise Physiology (CSEP) advises no more than two hours of recreational screen time a day, along with sixty minutes of physical activity and adequate sleep.[29] The American Academy of Pediatrics (AAP) suggests parents place consistent time limits on media use, prioritize sleep and physical activity, and use their family media plan to develop healthy media habits. Research shows that increased mental and physical health-related concerns are more likely with three or more hours of recreational media per day.[30] [31]

What Can We Do

* Develop deeper relationships with your Chrisitan friends by engaging in face-to-face interactions. Put your phone away while you're interacting in person. Eye contact increases empathy and helps you bond, and it shows that you value and respect that individual.

* Set daily screen time limits for entertainment use on your device. Spending too much time on technology can affect your sleep and mood, and distract you from your relationship with God. That's why experts recommend limiting non-educational use to no more than two hours per day. Use tracking apps like Bark, Google Family Link, or Flipd to help you stick to the limits you set.

❀ Delay daily entertainment screen use until you've given God time in His Word.

❀ Don't get social media platforms until you're <u>at least</u> sixteen years old. Social media can be a great way to connect with friends, but it can also be addictive and make you feel like you need to constantly compare yourself to others. Waiting until you're a little older to start using social media can help you avoid some of these challenges. And if you've already set up an account, there's no rule that says you can't deactivate it for a few years!

❀ Turn off all notifications and delete as many apps as you can on your phone to reduce distractions and improve focus.

❀ When you get home from school, put your phone on the kitchen counter. You'll find that if you keep your phone out of sight and out of reach, you won't feel the urge to check it at every moment of downtime.

❀ Designate media-free times together like when you're at dinner, participating in outdoor activities, or engaging in casual conversation. Try to have a conversation with your family instead of watching YouTube or scrolling Instagram while you're eating or spending time outdoors.

❀ Designate your bedroom as a media-free location. You'll find there's far less temptation to make poor choices when you're surrounded by others while using your device. Your sleep quality will be much better, too. *Newsflash: They actually still sell alarm clocks on Amazon—you don't HAVE to use your phone.*

If Time Equals Importance

Take a moment to consider your level of devotion to God compared to your device. Some of you check your phones up to 344 times per day. Are you giving even half that attention to God? A quarter of it, perhaps? I'd guess that many aren't dedicating any time to God daily. Proverbs 7:2-3 instructs us to "keep my commandments and live, and my teaching as the apple of your eye. Bind them on your fingers; write them on the tablet of your heart." In Joshua 1:8, we are told to meditate on God's law day and night. And in John 14:15, Jesus equates love to obeying His commandments. Girls, how can we know what God's commandments are if we aren't in His Word? We have Christians, even adults, who can navigate the internet like software engineers but struggle to find three verses on salvation or locate a book of the Bible without using their phone!

Do we honestly believe God is going to be satisfied with our commitment to Him if we spend hours on social media but can't spare even ten minutes for His Word? We must do better at maintaining purity in this area. I struggled with this a few years ago, spending hours on social media but neglecting God. So, I took Facebook off my phone (*best decision ever!*), and I made a rule for myself: I couldn't get on social media unless I had done my Bible reading for the day. I even set alarms as a reminder. It helped me so much! Maybe you have other techniques that work for you, like finding an accountability partner. Whatever it takes, let's be more committed to God than to our devices.

It's Time for Reflection!

1. After learning more about how technology impacts the brain and influences your behaviors, what changes do you need to implement?

2. Have you experienced many of the symptoms or behaviors identified as red flags for a screen addiction?

3. Identify and develop a plan in which you can better maintain purity with technology, then write it below. Turn off notifications, take off apps, and give yourself time limits on social media each day. It may include reaching out to a professional who can help you meet your goals.

This week, I want you to find time each day to get awkward and do the uncomfortable, by engaging in face-to-face interactions without a device in hand. Take a walk with your family, ride bikes, or just have a casual conversation with friends. You'll likely find your overall happiness and contentment in life will be much improved.

Chapter 7

Delving into the Influence of Tech on Sexual Immorality

✔ ❤ ❤ ❤ ✔ ❤ ❤ ❤ ❤ ✔ ❤ ❤ ❤ ❤ ✔ ❤ ❤

When I was working as a therapist with children in foster care, I met a sixteen-year-old girl, "Natalie," whose story has always stuck with me. When Natalie was in middle school, a classmate passed out notes to her friends with a website listed and told them to check it out. As a curious preteen, Natalie decided to see what it was about. That was Natalie's introduction to porn. Unfortunately, Natalie didn't have caregivers who talked with her about the dangers of pornography and how to protect yourself when you unintentionally see it. By the time I met her at sixteen, Natalie's addiction had gotten so severe that she was into hardcore porn and even bestiality (that's having a sexual relationship with animals). Seems crazy, right?! For many of us, our brains can't even fathom going that deep into sin. How does this happen? Keep reading, and I'll try to give you some insight on how technology can play a role in this downward slide into sin and addiction. I also hope to share some wisdom on how to beat this as you interact with a more and more "addicted" culture, even in the church.

Sexuality in the Age of Technology

In today's digital age, technology has a significant influence on our attitudes and behaviors, particularly when it comes to our sexual desires. The widespread use of smartphones has shifted the way we consume and think about sex, and has made it easy to access sexual pictures and videos whenever and wherever we want. One of the largest porn websites in the world recently published statistics revealing that smartphones contribute to a staggering 84 percent of their traffic.[1] It should be no surprise, then, that the younger generations like yours are increasingly consuming pornographic content.[2] The normalization of porn in mainstream culture has made it more accessible, with greater variety, and more socially acceptable than ever before.

However, technology hasn't normalized just porn. With the rise of social media platforms and messaging apps, it's easier than ever for teens to be exposed to sexually-explicit content or to engage in risky behaviors. The latest statistics indicate most of the sexting happens around age fifteen, with one in four teens receiving sexually-explicit texts.[3] Online social media platforms are even encouraging girls to send pictures of their bodies in exchange for easy cash—the more you show, the more you make (do not try this!). This further increases pressure to engage in sexual behavior. Given the ease of access to sexual content, what are you doing with it today and how is it affecting you?

The Prevalence of Pornography

Did you know that the United States is the top consumer of pornography globally?[4] With over 4.5 million porn sites available on our smartphones, it's no wonder that almost half of all high school girls say they've seen porn at least once.[56] Even if you haven't actively sought it out, chances are you might be like the 58 percent of teens who were unintentionally exposed.[7] I recently spoke with a sweet preteen who shared a horrifying experience of a pornographic advertisement popping up while she was streaming an innocent movie about sports. Although she was disgusted by what she observed, she said, "I can't get the image out of my head." Isn't that exactly what porn does? It has a way of searing that image in the brain. Most likely, if you've seen porn, you can remember the exact day, time, and location in which you were first exposed.

The use of smartphones, sexual content on the internet,

and media featuring attractive bodies in suggestive ways have made porn addictions more common for both genders. It used to be thought of as a problem mainly for guys, but now girls are getting involved, too. In the eight years from 2014 to 2022, female consumers of pornography on one of the largest porn websites worldwide increased by 13 percent.[8] In light of this, it's understandable that 36 percent of females regularly engage with it, when the media bombards us with soft porn on social media and makes us believe it's a normal part of life.[9] Some girls feel comfortable viewing porn because they think they can remain "anonymous" on the internet. However, it's important to realize that nothing we do on the internet is truly anonymous or private. As Luke 8:17 reminds us: "For nothing is concealed that will not become evident, nor anything hidden that will not be known and come to light." Even if you believe you've hidden or deleted inappropriate content, it's important to remember that everything will eventually be brought to light, whether on earth or in eternity.

Because the person watching pornography is the customer, these images are purposely made to be easy to find and available to as many people as possible. Companies that create and distribute this material are only concerned with making money and further promoting this content. One of the keys to their success is using algorithms to learn about what you like and recommend similar but equally as addictive content to keep you coming back. Not only do these companies make millions and millions of dollars each year, but they also thrive because they track who you are and then can sell your information to other companies. **Your online activity is not anonymous!** The success of these companies depends on knowing what you do, what you look at, and how you respond. This is part of the formula to trap you in the cycle of addiction. That is why when you see one inappropriate reel on Tik Tok—accidentally or not—the algorithms are designed to keep offering those types of videos in your feed, pulling you in further and making it harder to resist and avoid future viewing.

The Lies Pornography Tells

Society is on the slippery slope of sexual destruction and walking further from the Lord in the process. This may be because what society considers pornographic has drastically changed. An alarming number of teens don't consider sexual imagery or graphic nudity to be porn unless it depicts sexual intercourse. This contrasts with Matthew 5:28, where it warns, "But I say to you that everyone who looks at a woman *[this principle applies to both men and women]* with lust for her has already committed adultery with her in his heart." Give it time, and much of what you consider "pornography" today will be viewed as normal. We risk losing our sense of shame.

It's important to understand that pornography paints a wildly-unrealistic picture of what godly, committed relationships should look like. In fact, the messages conveyed by porn are completely different from the values taught in the Bible. Here are some of the common lies of pornography:

- Porn is a realistic image of intimacy.
- You can have no-strings-attached sex.
- Everyone my age views porn.
- Porn doesn't change who I am.

Repeatedly viewing pornography can cause us to believe what we see on the internet is common behavior. A 2023 Common Sense Media study found that 84 percent of the pornographic images viewed by youth depict acts of violence, rape, and choking someone in pain.[10] It's becoming both aggressive and humiliating. These images are not only unnatural, but they also begin to influence you to believe this is how sexual relationships should be. That's likely why over a third of girls report pornography as a realistic depiction of sex.[11] Don't believe it! These are Satan's lies! In Ephesians 5, Paul urges husbands to love their wives as Christ loved the church. He elaborates further to encourage men to love, cherish, and nourish their wives as they do their own bodies. Pornography could not be further from what God desires in a committed marriage relationship.

Pornography objectifies and lessens your value as a woman. Porn makes you believe you can have sex without emotional connection, responsibility, or intimacy. It teaches that two people use sex for momentary "fun" rather than as an expression of love. Going against what the Bible teaches us about sexual intimacy has consequences for your physical and emotional wellbeing. It will cause you to walk away from what should be a beautiful interaction between a couple, leaving you feeling empty and burdened with mental health issues. Hebrews 13:4 records that "Marriage is to be held in honor among all, and the marriage bed is to be undefiled." Sex is a beautiful expression of love that God intended for many purposes, but unfortunately, it's often used in ways that go against His design (read Chapter 10 to learn more about God's design for sex!). Beware of the deceptive tactics of the serpent who tries to twist God's Word by asking, "Certainly God didn't mean sex was ONLY for marriage?" Don't let porn ruin what God created to build and strengthen the committed relationship of marriage.

Porn's Addictive Nature

Porn is destroying your brain. I'm not exaggerating! Numerous studies have shown that viewing pornography is highly addictive, so it's not shocking that many teens are using it, especially considering how easily available it is. Porn use can cause the prefrontal cortex (the upstairs part of the brain responsible for decision-making and willpower) to shrink.[12] This makes it harder for you to make good choices. Pornography can also affect your body image, leading to a destructive pattern of thoughts and behaviors that cause you to hate your body. A study from Franciscan University of Steubenville on Compulsive Internet Pornography Use and Mental Health found that girls who watch porn experience significantly higher levels of stress, depression, and anxiety.[13]

Remember our conversation about the pleasure chemical dopamine in the last chapter? When you use porn, it triggers a release of dopamine. In fact, it turns up the brain's dopamine production as high as it will go, which often leads to addiction.[14] Similar to how a smoker may start with just one cigarette and quickly escalate to two packs a day, you may already have found yourself needing to watch more and more porn to achieve that same feeling of pleasure. You'll notice that the same thing you viewed the first time just isn't doing it for you anymore. This can lead to cravings for more and makes it hard to stop watching. This is why pornography has become increasingly more extreme and perverse. For example, do you know what the suggested video content currently includes on one of the world's largest porn sites? Incestuous relationships![15] Why would they encourage relationships that are both disturbing and disgusting to the average person? Because their consumers have already become desensitized to other forms of sexual content. Remember what happened to Natalie? It doesn't take long for sin to take you further than you ever intended to go! Satan has told these LIES to every young girl who has considered looking at porn— "Just once won't hurt" or "Just once won't make you addicted." This is a dangerous way of thinking that has led to the addiction of many. As the Bible says, "flee sexual immorality" (1 Corinthians 6:18).

Let's Talk About Sexting

Teens are increasingly considering sexting, which includes sending, receiving, or forwarding sexually explicit photos, messages, or videos of full- or partial-nudity, a *normal* part of their dating relationships. Our culture glorifies sexual experiences outside of marriage as a common, positive, and fun way to connect with your partner. And society isn't doing anything to help by bombarding you with lies about these behaviors. Spot the lie:

> "Sexting is totally healthy and fun...You can try a lot
> of things on your sex menu virtually before you make
> those dreams really come true."[16]
> ~Karen Fratti

It's understandable, then, that over 50 percent of young people have taken a naked selfie and shared it with someone else.[17] If you're using your phone to send sexts, know that it will have many damaging effects. Although the world may say that as long as it's consensual there's no harm, that's just not true! In fact, sexting as a minor is a criminal offense that could land you a misdemeanor or felony charge in many states. This aspect of sexting is often completely ignored by social media platforms. Could you imagine the embarrassment of going to jail over an illicit text you thought no one would see? Is it really worth the risk?

The Scars of Sexting

The consequences of sexting are overwhelming and underestimated! Understand that you do not owe any man naked pictures of yourself for them to stay with you! What kind of man are you seeking to attract? If a guy demands naked pics as a sign of commitment, is he genuinely someone who'll love and respect you? What will he do when a slightly more attractive girl catches his eye? Imagine if your boyfriend, post break-up, decides to share your private images, or worse, posts them online for everyone to view? The humiliation, shame, and damage to your reputation may be so severe that it triggers symptoms of anxiety and depression. There are countless stories of girls' lives being ruined simply because they started sending what they thought were harmless nude pictures.

Girls, I cannot emphasize enough what I've already said in this chapter—what you do in private with technology NEVER truly disappears. Now is the time to be too embarrassed to even take that photo. Sexting can have lifelong consequences, scarring you emotionally, damaging your reputation, and causing embarrassment and humiliation for both you and your future husband. Intimate images that were meant to be reserved for a covenant relationship should not be shared and enjoyed by countless strangers or perverts.

Sexting can cause severe emotional scars, but the spiritual consequences are even worse. These behaviors could cost you eternal separation from your Creator. According to Colossians 3:5, we should, "Therefore, treat the parts of your earthly body as dead *to* sexual immorality, impurity, passion, evil desire, and greed, which amounts to idolatry." As Christian girls, we should completely rid ourselves of sexual immorality by avoiding sexting, since it cannot be done in a pure and God-honoring way. Rather than giving into our fleshly desires, we should "honor God with our bodies" (1 Corinthians 6:20). It's not worth risking eternity over—just don't do it! Because sexting has become so prevalent in our society, I'm sure that some of you are already doing this. Forgiving yourself can be the hardest, but one of the most important, steps to beating this sin. You can conquer this! Talk with your mother or an older spiritual woman who can help you through this. They love you and want nothing more than for you to spend eternity with them in Heaven. Remember, "…with God all things are possible" (Matthew 19:26).

How To Overcome Sexual Addiction

Are you ready to follow a plan to reclaim purity in this area? Great! The first step to overcoming any sin we've allowed to slip into our lives is the desire to quit. In fact, 81 percent of individuals who successfully conquered pornography addiction recognized their own motivation as the primary factor in their ability to quit.[18] To break the cycle of sexual sin, you'll have to build a line of defense with your eyes, mind, and heart.[19] Start with your eyes. Identify and name inappropriate sexual content when you see it. Are there certain media apps, online platforms, or shows that affect your sexual drive and encourage these behaviors? When you go to your favorite social media platform, do you turn to that one person, picture, or picture source that you know is a real temptation? It may require you saying to yourself, "That's pornography. I'm not participating in that!" Get rid of those triggers! When something unexpected pops up on your phone, bounce your eyes or turn your head and visualize a "Keep Out" sign in your mind. Distracting yourself during those moments may help you in overcoming the desire to look.

Once you've put the padlock on the door by getting rid of triggers that cause you to participate in sexual sin, don't ever loosen it back up! First Peter 5:8 tells us that the devil "…prowls around like a roaring lion, seeking someone to devour." Don't take that padlock off by going back to old habits, because the devil is happily waiting to pounce on you! This starts out as very difficult and you will fail from time to time, but it does get easier—stay determined to bounce your eyes until it becomes and feels natural. May I suggest that you don't keep your phone in the room at night? We tend to let our guard down when it's late and we're alone, behind closed doors. If you struggle with pornography, I'd highly recommend you go smartphone free as well. They make cute, smartphone lookalikes that allow you to text and call but do not have access to the internet. You'll find the path to purity will be much more attainable if you add this "padlock." When Cain had fallen into sin, God told him, "Sin is crouching at the door; and its desire is for you, but you must master it" (Genesis 4:7). Part of ruling over sexual sin is to put the appropriate boundaries in place so you overcome it.

Second, train your mind to maintain control of your thoughts as we are instructed in 2 Corinthians 10:5. When you feel compelled to send that nude picture to your boyfriend or watch something you know is sinful, set up a line of defense in your mind. Don't dwell on thoughts that pull you into sin but replace them with scripture like 1 Corinthians 10:13, "No temptation has overtaken you except something common to mankind; and God is faithful, so He will not allow you to be tempted beyond what you are able, but with the temptation will provide the way of escape also, so that you will be able to endure it."

It all begins with recognizing the moment you feel the urge to engage in behaviors that go against what you know is right. By taking control of your sexual desires, you can express them in a way that is beautiful, fulfilling, and in alignment with Jesus' teachings. With practice, you can learn to control your desires and express them in a way that Jesus would approve of.

Your third line of defense will be the heart. Proverbs 4:23 says, "Watch over your heart with all diligence, for from it flow the springs of life." You must have a heart that desires to serve

God over self. Overcoming sexual addiction is not a quick fix and it's going to require patience and persistence. Seek Christian friends and spiritual mentors who share your values and can provide support as you journey towards healing. Remember, you are not alone in this struggle. Many Christians have faced similar challenges and have found freedom and healing. With determination, support, and a plan of action, you can overcome sexual addiction and live a life of purity and wholeness.

It's Time for Reflection!

1. Take some time this week to reflect and journal on the areas you are allowing sexual sin to invade your life through technology.

2. Keep a daily record of your triggers and patterns for participating in these behaviors.

   Are there certain apps or social media platforms that are encouraging this behavior? What times or places do you feel most compelled to view or participate in these things?

3. Pray about having the heart to make the changes required to rediscover purity in this area. No matter what sexual sins you've given into, you can break free from them! Pray for guidance and strength. Seek support from your spiritual mentors. You are not alone. You can rediscover purity through the lens of your Creator!

Chapter 8

Attending School Dances and Your Impact on Others

♥ ♥ ♥ ♥ ♥ ♥ ♥ ♥ ♥ ♥ ♥ ♥ ♥ ♥ ♥ ♥ ♥

As a teenager, media, friends, and family overwhelm you with messages about what you should and shouldn't do, which can make it challenging to know what's right. One area that often sparks debate is attending a school dance. When it comes to attending school dances, you've probably heard a lot of different opinions from your parents, teachers, and church leaders. But, have you ever stopped to ask yourself what God might think about it?

During my adolescent years, I heard quite a few lessons on school dances and why a Christian wouldn't want to go. I even attended a prom alternative or two. But, it wasn't until my senior year of high school that I felt the pull to attend *what seemed to be* the most significant event of high school. The guy I'd had a crush on since ninth grade asked me to prom. I was so excited to be asked, but at the same time, I felt heartbroken because of the conflicting messages I'd heard about attending dances. I still remember sobbing in my bed as I talked with my mom about how I desperately wanted to go but felt torn on what to do. After pouring my heart out to her, my mom told me she'd let me make the decision (she may have been a bit of a softie on her little girl).

Most parents today really don't see an issue with letting their kids attend school dances. School dances are fun! You get to dress up and look pretty. So, you might be asking yourself, does it really matter if I attend the school dance? What's the big deal? As we'll explore in this chapter, there are a lot of reasons why attending a school dance IS a big deal.

The Dress

Let's start with the attire at high school dances. Is there a different standard of clothing when you are at a formal activity? First Timothy 2:9 admonishes women "to adorn themselves with proper clothing, modestly and discreetly." Do the dresses at high school dances violate the standard for "proper clothing"? Most are too tight, too revealing, too short, and too suggestive. Formal-wear advertisers encourage girls to wear "sultry, sexy style" dresses with midriffs showing and open backs that literally have slits all the way to the hip to "make heads turn" when you walk into prom.[1] We've already talked about how males and females think differently, and that guys' brains are wired to respond strongly to what they see. Studies have shown that boys tend to pay more attention to appearance and may be more likely to be inappropriately aroused by things they see.[2] Are we encouraging our male counterparts to lust and stumble in their faith when we dress in tight, short, skimpy dresses that leave almost nothing to the imagination?

Furthermore, do we really want to support an event we know will make it difficult for guys pursuing godliness to remain pure in their thoughts? Remember, you are to set the example "in speech, conduct, love, faith, and purity" (1 Timothy 4:12). If you invite your friends to youth group activities or Bible study but then look (and maybe even act) like the non-Christian girls in your school, what will separate you from them? What will those you are trying to influence for God see in you that is different, unique, or righteous?

Prom—How the World Identifies It

To many, prom is an iconic part of the traditional high school experience. It's glamorized in the movies as one of the most magical nights of your life. If you're watching one of these movies, you're likely to catch a steamy scene of what often goes on during the afterparty with the couple. Our culture has promoted prom as a rite of passage from adolescence to adulthood. It's become such a momentous event that many of your moms dream about and anxiously anticipate a "prom proposal" for you.

It only takes a quick Google search on prom to find out what it's synonymous for—sex. If you're reading this and thinking, "I've never considered that before" or "I've never heard about prom and sex being connected," remember that the rest of the world may not see it the same way as you. "One prom pressure far outweighs the rest: I'm talking about having sex for the first time. Or at least the cultural expectation that you need to have sex on this very specific night," says Splinter News.[3] MTV News also associates prom with losing your virginity. "It's a night that's been built up since basically forever, in countless movies and magazine articles."[4] PopSugar produced an article titled, "8 Things to Know if You Want to Lose Your Virginity on Prom Night."[5] Clearly, there's a strong connection in the world between sex and prom. But if that isn't enough, let's talk about the after party. Many students attend the after party, which has become known for sex, drugs, and alcohol. One popular blog advertises that at prom after parties there is no extreme censorship on music played, so you can have "pure uninhibited fun like anyone else at the club" with "no prying eyes."[6] But even if you leave out the fact that prom is often known for losing your virginity or participating in other sinful behaviors, there's some other things that need to be considered.

Dancing

If you know anything about prom, you know the main event is dancing! However, the kind of dancing that takes place at prom and other high school dances is not the sweet and innocent "five-year-old girl twirling around in the living room" kind of dancing. Instead, it's sexually suggestive and sinful. A Christian friend who has supervised prom as an educator once told me *(paraphrased)*, "Anyone who supports school dances and calls themselves a Christian probably hasn't seen what goes on there—or at least I would hope that's why they still let their children attend these events." If you're a mama reading this chapter, I'd encourage you to ask a faithful Christian who has staffed these events their take on the dancing that goes on there.

In Galatians 5:19, the Bible warns against "sexual immorality, impurity and indecent behavior," all of which will keep someone out of the kingdom of Heaven. Indecent behavior is also condemned in Mark 7:22 and 2 Corinthians 12:21. So, what exactly is "indecent behavior"? The Greek word for indecent behavior, *aselgeia,* refers to "unbridled lust, lasciviousness, wantonness, indecent bodily movements, and unchaste handling of males and females, etc."[7] This includes any form of dancing outside of marriage that draws attention to body parts pertaining to sexuality. "Unchaste handling of males and females" involves touching or rubbing body areas sensitive to sexual stimulation. The activities described don't require a bedroom or closed doors. Actually, many of them happen in high school gymnasiums across the United States. Girls, if you knew someone was recording you during your school dance to show your youth group or post on social media, you'd probably be ashamed. Let me encourage you to feel that same shame and embarrassment beforehand and avoid going to the dance in the first place.

Okay! I Won't Dance, I'll Just Watch

Prom and high school dances are particularly problematic because they involve teens whose hormones and lack of maturity make it difficult to maintain pure thoughts. Dancing that is sexual in nature creates lust, and what does lust do? "It gives birth to sin" (James 1:15). King Herod and Herodias provide a good biblical example of how watching sexually-suggestive dancing can affect a person's judgment and produce negative consequences. In the book of Mark, it says:

> "An opportune day came when Herod, on his birthday, held a banquet for his nobles and military commanders, and the leading people of Galilee; and when the daughter of Herodias herself came in and danced, she pleased Herod and his dinner guests; and the king said to the girl, "Ask me for whatever you want, and I will give it to you." And he swore to her, "Whatever you ask of me, I will give it to you, up to half of my kingdom" (Mark 6:21-23).

Let's take a moment to think about this, girls. Do you really believe a man would be willing to give away half of everything he owns just to see someone dance with no sexual suggestion and no revealing clothes? It's foolish to think anything other than the promise of sexual fulfillment swayed the king. Later, he realized he had made a mistake by promising her so much; his desire for her had clouded his judgment. This biblical story illustrates how "just" watching sexually-stimulating dancing can affect a person's judgment and cause them to do things they wouldn't normally do.

The Music

In addition to sexually-suggestive dancing, prom is filled with sexually-explicit music that further encourages couples to get "in the mood." Don't believe me? Try searching the "Top Five Prom Songs" and read the lyrics. Most of them are so offensive and vulgar, I can't quote them here; they definitely encourage sexual, promiscuous behavior. This begs the question: Why do so many young people insist prom is not about sex, it's about [insert every other excuse made to attend the event here]? Studies have revealed a correlation between sexually-explicit lyrics and risky sexual behaviors.[8] When you go to an event filled with sexually-arousing music and dancing, you are begging for trouble and flirting with the temptation to sin. As Christians, we are called to "flee immorality" (1 Corinthians 6:18) and "abstain from fleshly lusts, which wage war against the soul" (1 Peter 2:11). Christians should not attend any event that revolves around or promotes sinful activities! We may feel awkward, and the conversations may be uncomfortable with our friends, but we absolutely must be willing to take a stand.

Your Image

Does it matter to you what image you portray to the world around you? I've heard many people try to justify going to dances with things like,

- I'm not going for the dance.
- I'm not going to do what they do there.
- I'm only going for the pictures.
- I'm going to "be the light" in the dark world.

First Thessalonians 5:22 tells us to "abstain from every form *(or appearance)* of evil." If you attend prom using a common justification like the ones above, I have just a few questions for you to consider. Do your social media followers know you don't agree with the dancing, sex, or alcohol use that happens at prom? Some of you argue you go just for the pictures. But, if you have to put a caveat on any picture you post on social media, there is a problem! Y'all, this same theology says, "I'm only going to Hooters for the wings." Or it says, "I'm only going to a night-club to be a good example to others there—I won't drink, dance, or look at the inappropriately-dressed women."

As a Christian, you are married to the Lord. Can you look Him in the face and say, "I'm going somewhere where I might risk breaking our covenant relationship, but only to take pictures, God?" Or perhaps, "Lord, I love you, but being socially accepted means more to me than preserving my purity and influence for Your cause!" What would His response be to, "Lord, I know you told me when we were joined together through baptism that I should flee these sorts of things, but it's too much fun and everyone else is doing it?"

Let me say it once more: any time there is an event where the primary activity is inherently sinful, Christians shouldn't be going. Your attendance is not abstinence from "every appearance of evil." There are no extra stars in your heavenly crown for those who've deliberately put themselves in super tempting or sinful situations and came out without sinning. There's only the dimming of your influence, the staining of your reputation, and the glorification of self over the Savior. Matthew 5:16 states, "Your light must shine before people in such a way that they may see your good works, and glorify your Father who is in heaven." When you go to prom, it's not being the light—it's conforming to the world. I'm grateful I had spiritual mentors as a teen to challenge me to think about the activities I participated in. It's why I made the decision not to go. I hope you will, too, even if your parents think otherwise. Don't straddle the fence here, but instead, stand up for the sake of purity!

It's Time for Reflection!

1. Some of the information you read during this chapter may be new to you. Please keep an open mind as you consider this important topic. I know it's tempting to dismiss topics that may seem insignificant to us, but it's imperative to look at what principles the Bible teaches on these topics. Take time this week to reflect on what you've read. Reread the scriptures presented in this chapter and write out the pros and cons to why you should or shouldn't attend the dance.

2. Remember, just because you choose not to attend prom or other high school dances doesn't mean you can't get dressed up and do something enjoyable with your friends! What are some other entertaining prom alternatives you could suggest to your church leaders? You could organize a formal dinner, attend a theme park, go on an outdoor adventure, or arrange a special night with other churches in your area. You can still have good, clean fun! Come up with a few ideas and present them to your youth leaders this week.

Chapter 9

Understanding the LGBTQ+ Movement

♥ ♥ ♥ ♥ ♥ ♥ ♥ ♥ ♥ ♥ ♥ ♥ ♥ ♥ ♥ ♥ ♥

"Loving everyone for who they are
is exactly what you should do."[1]
~ JoJo Siwa

With just a momentary glance at popular TV sitcoms and commercials, online video sharing, or social media platforms, you can see how our society is trying to slowly desensitize you to the LGBTQ+ movement. We live in a culture where teen pop sensations are being labeled as "brave" and "courageous" for coming out as queer.[2] As a teen growing up in American culture, there's no doubt you've been exposed to an abundance of LGBTQ+-friendly entertainment and media. Is it just me, or does it puzzle you, too, that giant corporations, the government, and celebrities hand out a significant amount of money and resources to promote and embrace a lifestyle that represents only 1.4 percent of the young people in the United States?[3] When I was growing up, these behaviors were highly uncommon. My generation embraced the ideas presented in verses like Mark 10:6, acknowledging that from the beginning of creation God "created them male and female." However, in today's world, there's no longer any shame in blatantly disregarding God's design for man and woman.

The promotion of the LBGTQ+ agenda started as toddlers for many of you when seemingly innocent TV shows began adding homosexual characters for your viewing pleasure. Many in the LGBTQ+ community have developed books, games, and other activities that encourage inclusive environments and celebrate differences in an effort to capture the hearts of young children. It makes perfect sense, then, why Scholastic chose a book from the LGBTQ+ reading list to give out to my daughter's Pre-K class and why the school took four-year-olds on a field trip to a play on gender roles. You absolutely cannot get away from it and, as you get older, the agenda is no longer quite as subtle. While my ten-year-old daughter was casually enjoying music on YouTube, what did this incredibly popular online video sharing platform—with its staggering monthly user count of over two billion—decide to endorse to its young viewers?[4] They promoted "The Gay Quiz" and displayed a graphic featuring an elementary school child expressing the thought, "I think I might be gay." It's no surprise homosexuality and transgenderism are becoming very popular behaviors among your peers and why you really aren't shocked by what you see anymore.

Because the current cultural craze seems to focus primarily on transgenderism, I'll give special attention to it during this chapter. Transgenderism refers to a person who does not identify with their biological sex.[5] A person who identifies as transgender often experiences gender dysphoria, which is defined as a severe or persistent discomfort with one's biological sex.[6] Although it's become a trendy identity to embrace, historically, gender dysphoria was only observed in about .01 percent of the population, primarily among boys.[7] Prior to 2012, there were no scientific publications indicating any diagnosis of gender dysphoria among girls aged eleven to twenty-one![8] For the first time in medical history, girls are not only identifying as transgender, but they also represent the majority.[9]

The United States has experienced a significant rise in the number of teens diagnosed with gender dysphoria. The most recent four years of available data indicate that while the overall population growth has been minimal, the occurrence of gender dysphoria has increased dramatically. At first, the average growth over three years was 18 percent. But lately, the rate of increase has skyrocketed to nearly 70 percent each year, showing a major jump in how fast it's growing.[10] A recent UCLA Williams Institute of Law study estimated that the transgender youth population has <u>almost doubled</u> in the last five years.[11] But this isn't just happening in the United States—the trans movement is happening in many developed countries around the world.

You may be wondering, what has caused the transgender craze we currently seem to be experiencing in the United States? For starters, there's no such thing as a tomboy anymore. Very young girls are being diagnosed with gender dysphoria because they exhibit various signs like: a strong desire to identify as a different gender, a preference for masculine clothing and toys traditionally associated with boys, a desire to play the male role in imaginative play, a preference for male playmates, a rejection of feminine toys and activities, and discomfort with one's own biological sex characteristics.[12] For decades, people thought young girls who desired to wear shorts and T-shirts were less "girly," not gay or trans. This is completely normal based on your personal preference and certainly should not raise any red flags about your identity. As for preferring boy playmates, games, and activities, here's how I see it: if you're like me and grew up with only brothers, you played a lot more baseball than Barbie dolls. Personally, I found it easier to play with boys than girls, because they're a whole lot less dramatic.

Regarding playing with "boy" toys—again, why does society get to determine this means you are likely experiencing gender identity issues? And why are they only just now calling this an identity issue when for so many years this has been normal? What changed? It makes no sense! This is very normal behavior based on the gender of your siblings, your environment, and who raised you. So, you may already have thoughts like, "I'm not normal because I don't like dresses" or "I'd rather play video games than play with baby dolls," and then you hit puberty. Your hormones are out of control and you don't feel comfortable in your body. Of course you're going to start to question who and what you are when everyone around you suggests you're abnormal. Again, your entertainment choices, toy preferences, and who you choose as friends have everything to do with your family dynamics, cultural environment, and the geographic location in which you live. It is both perverted and sinful to convince you it's anything other!

Unveiling Cultural Influences: Navigating Messages About Identity

So, what exactly is culture teaching you? Well, our culture is trying to get you to question every aspect of your gender and identity. Just consider the constant stream of messages you receive from the entertainment media you consume each day. At the time I researched for the writing of this chapter, there were over one hundred YouTube channels focused exclusively on transgenderism.[13] If you checked today, I bet you would find this number has already increased! Imagine the impact popular LGBTQ+ YouTubers with over 4.5 billion views and 23 million subscribers are having on their viewing audience![14] You may be one of their subscribers yourself. If so, just think about how it has affected you.

Many of the stories I've read about those who have undergone gender transition mentioned that they stumbled across a YouTube channel dedicated to transgender topics, became captivated, and started binge-watching its content. You've got trans influencers who are asking questions like,

- Are you not really fitting in?
- Do you feel different?
- Are you feeling uncomfortable in your body?[15]
- Do you feel like your body doesn't match you/how you feel?
- When you were younger, did you like to pretend to be or dress up as a different gender?
- Do you feel like your gender assigned at birth doesn't fit you?
- Think you might be transgender? You are loved and valued as you are, for who you are.[16]

If you answer yes to these kinds of questions, these influencers wholeheartedly affirm that you might be transgender. They celebrate transgender experiences and advocate for the use of cross-sex hormones (or worse!). However, they don't present all the potential challenges that arise from living an LGBTQ+ lifestyle, nor do they encourage a healthy understanding of your innate desires and how you were uniquely created by God.

Don't buy into these lies because, ultimately, you will never find genuine happiness in this lifestyle.

Unveiling the Truth: Government Influence & Gender Affirming Care

Psalm 139:13 beautifully reveals the incredible wisdom of God in creating us perfectly, just as we are, stating, "For you created my innermost parts; you wove me in my mother's womb." While many Christians embrace this truth, society often fails to understand its significance. Currently, there is a strong push from the government, psychologists, and the LGBTQ+ community to encourage teenagers, like you, to embrace and accept identities that do not align with God's creation. President Biden made history by establishing the Transgender Day of Visibility and delivered a message to young people, saying, "Just be you. You are heard. You are understood. You do belong."[17]

Society is actively supporting the LGBTQ+ culture by endorsing gender affirming care. If you're unfamiliar with the term, gender affirming care is a treatment approach meant to "support" young individuals facing distress due to their gender identity. It involves social transition, hormone therapy, and possibly surgery to alter or remove body parts. While the United States is aggressively advocating for gender affirming care, other countries like Sweden, France, Australia, and New Zealand take a more cautious approach. These countries believe that puberty blockers and hormone treatment could be more harmful than helpful for minors.

What are some important aspects of gender affirming care that its supporters may not be sharing with you? To begin with, puberty blockers given to children "can have dangerous side effects, including lowered bone density, stunted growth, and permanent infertility."[18] Additionally, studies have shown that a significant number of children with gender dysphoria do not continue to experience these feelings as they grow older. Actually, highly respected psychologists have found that roughly 85 percent of kids with gender dysphoria do not continue to experience it as they grow into their teens![19] It should be both disturbing and enraging to every one of you to know that life-altering PHYSICAL treatments are being used to address temporary MENTAL conditions! Society has determined that as a young person, you aren't mentally capable to get a tattoo, vote, marry, drink alcohol, or smoke *(the latter two you shouldn't do anyway)*, but this same group of people is encouraging you to permanently change your body. The very idea is appalling! I hope you can see the lies that are being presented to you.

Navigating Gender Identity and Mental Health: A Critical Examination

You may be familiar with Jazz Jennings, a well-known figure in the media, particularly for his TLC television series, *I Am Jazz.* His mother claimed Jazz showed signs of gender identity issues as early as age two, mentioning how he tried to undo buttons on his onesies to make them look like a dress.[20] Is this not one of the most outrageous things you've ever heard? I'm pretty sure every one of my kiddos were immediately unpopping those seemingly endless buttons just as soon as I got them all fastened. And trust me, their button-popping frenzy had absolutely nothing to do with gender dysphoria! They were just excited they had mastered the new skill. At the age of two, most children can only communicate in two-to-three-word phrases and lack the cognitive ability to understand anything about gender. Despite this, doctors diagnosed Jazz with gender dysphoria at age four and, supported by his parents, he transitioned to a girl by age five, accompanied by media attention and glamorization. In a 2013 interview, Bar-

bara Walters referred to Jazz as the "brave and beautiful new face of a child born in the wrong body."[21]

Did you know that across the United States, mental health professionals are being strongly encouraged to support young children like Jazz to feel comfortable with their sexual orientation and gender identity? Trying to help someone change or understand the cause of the gender confusion has been identified as "dangerous, discredited, and ineffective practices" by the experts.[22] Let's think about it logically: in no other area of life would we respond the same way. If a teen came into therapy claiming they were a frog, no *good* therapist would advocate for the parents to rush out to purchase a lily pad mattress, feed them flies, and allow them to croak as their new form of communication. That sounds ridiculous, right?! Similarly, if someone said, "I'm ugly," a therapist wouldn't support that feeling and suggest plastic surgery. Instead, they would help the individual work through their thoughts, emotions, and the underlying situations that led to those feelings.

In a study of patients who visited Oxford Gender Clinic with gender dysphoria, most of them experienced mental health issues, particularly depression.[23] This suggests that many individuals seeking help for gender dysphoria also struggle with their mental well-being. It's important to understand that people in distress may take drastic measures to improve their situation, as seen in the case of Chloe Cole, who underwent a double mastectomy at fifteen and was speaking out against it by eighteen years old. "Many of us were young teenagers when we decided, on the direction of medical experts, to pursue irreversible hormone treatments and surgeries. This is not informed consent but a decision forced under extreme duress," said Chloe.[24] Unfortunately, Jazz Jennings has faced various mental health issues as well, as revealed in a recent video confession where he expressed his struggle with self-understanding and happiness:

"I can't get out of my head. It doesn't stop. I feel all over the place. I want to be able to understand myself and be able to read my own soul and what I want. All I want is to be happy and to feel like me and I don't feel like me ever."[25]

Are you beginning to understand the situation better? Just because you experience changes in puberty and start feeling confused, this doesn't mean anything about the gender God assigned you! And if you recognize any key point from the previous discussion, I hope you realize that altering your body will only result in additional emotional challenges. Girls, if you're feeling uncertain with your identity, there are many factors that could be leading you that way. Renowned psychologist Dr. Kenneth Zucker, who ran a gender identity clinic for over thirty years, played a key role in defining gender dysphoria in the Diagnostic and Statistical Manual of Mental Disorders (DSM). Dr. Zucker discovered that childhood sexual abuse and trauma could contribute to children questioning their sexual preferences. He also found that about 88 percent of his clients who were not socially transitioned by their parents eventually outgrow their dysphoria.[26] It's important to recognize that societal influences, peer pressure, and the media you watch can also contribute to how you feel about yourself. Be true to what God created you to be instead of letting society define you; and remember that God's wisdom surpasses cultural norms (Isaiah 55:8-9).

Despite the picture culture paints, I believe there are far more transitioners whose feelings resemble Chloe and Jazz rather than those who find genuine happiness in living the trans life. You see, when you go against the nature of God, you will never feel complete. Jeremiah 29:11 assures us that God has a purpose and a plan for each of us, and only when we align ourselves with His will can we experience true fulfillment. I know it can be tough to feel comfortable in your own skin at times, and you might have some awkward questions or feelings you're hesitant to bring up with the adults in your life. Well, here's the thing: those questions and awkward moments are completely normal as you grow and change. They don't define who you are in Christ or as a person permanently. When you're feeling uneasy, take some time to talk to the King in prayer. Trust me, He gets it! He's willing to help and understands what you're going through. If you're struggling with these issues, I would also encourage you to seek guidance and support from a spiritual mentor in your church who can provide prayer and guidance in accordance with God's Word. This is something you can overcome! Don't let Satan tell you it's not worth fighting for. You are worth the fight!

LGBTQ+ from a Biblical Perspective

As a Christian, you may be wondering how to respond to the cultural shift towards acceptance of the LGBTQ+ lifestyle. Let me start by saying that everyone deserves to be treated with love and respect. Your friends who may truly feel like they are gay or trans need a response that is both honest and heartfelt. As followers of Christ, we don't hate those who claim to be LGBTQ+, but we do need to speak up with truthfulness and love as instructed through biblical teaching. First Corinthians 13:4 reminds us, "Love is patient, love is kind, it is not jealous; love does not brag, it is not arrogant." When you approach conversations with your friends about their chosen lifestyle, do it with kindness and gentleness. The Bible goes on to say that love "does not rejoice in unrighteousness, but rejoices with the truth" (13:6). As you discuss this important subject, rejoice in the truth of God's Word. Let your love for your neighbor motivate you to engage in these conversations. Sometimes tension arises when discussing the practice of sin. Remember, you can be vocal about sin while still being ruled by love. I will share a few realistic scenarios and offer some suggestions on what you can say to your friends.

• **Cynthia:** "I feel like I was born gay and I know God would want me to be happy, so you should accept me as I am!"

Response: There are many people in this world who feel like Cynthia. Here's where I would begin engaging in conversations with friends like her. The concept of homosexuality is not new; we can find references to it in various parts of the Bible. For example, in Genesis 19, we read about the men of the city of Sodom desiring sexual relationships with other men. Lot, recognizing the wickedness of their desires, pleaded with them not to act in that way (Genesis 19:7). Similarly, the city of Corinth was known for its sexual immorality, and even within the Church, there were individuals engaging in homosexual behavior. In 1 Corinthians 6:9-11, it states:

"Or do you not know that the unrighteous will not inherit the kingdom of God? Do not be deceived; neither the sexually immoral, nor idolaters, nor adulterers, nor homosexuals, nor thieves, nor the greedy, nor those habitually drunk, nor verbal abusers, nor swindlers, will inherit the kingdom of God. Such were some of you; but you were washed, but you were sanctified, but you were justified in the name of the Lord Jesus Christ and in the Spirit of our God."

My favorite part of this entire passage is, "Such were some of you." I find it so encouraging that there were people in the city of Corinth who had previously *chosen* a homosexual lifestyle who were convicted and able to change their ways! Isn't that wonderful? It wasn't a matter of genetics. While people may have tendencies or inclinations, God would not create us with conditions that would condemn us. God is a fair and loving

Father. This passage gives us hope that with God's help, we can overcome any sin or struggle.

• **Sandra:** "I've become increasingly more uncomfortable in my body and with who I am. Since I began researching transgenderism, I've decided that this identity fits me best. I've started dressing like a boy because it makes me feel better about myself. I want everyone to accept me unconditionally as a man, and my pronouns are he/him."

Response: It's important to address Sandra's feelings and experiences with empathy and understanding. However, we should also examine how God designed us from the beginning. In the creation account found in Genesis 1:27, we read that "God created man in His own image, in the image of God He created him; male and female He created them." God made us male and female, and each gender is unique and complementary. He designed us to reflect His image and called His creation "very good." Our bodies, therefore, are not our own; they represent our Creator.[27]

Now, let's explore the perspective of Andrew Sims, a contributor to Focus on the Family:

"Imagine receiving an original, priceless painting. Would you even consider getting your paints out and changing it? God not only created you but also sacrificed His Son to redeem you from sin and death. Altering healthy sexual organs denies that you are God's masterpiece and embraces the lie that your value and identity come from your appearance, preferences, and sexuality."[28]

It's crucial to understand that changing your appearance, genitalia, or hormones doesn't truly change your sex. Your biological sex, determined by your DNA, is an integral part of your God-given body. We cannot present our bodies as a "living and holy sacrifice, acceptable to God" (Romans 12:1) when we alter them in ways that God did not intend. Rejecting our bodies in this way goes against God's plan for us. Every aspect of our bodies is purposefully designed, some of which may not be fully understood yet.[29] Furthermore, altering your body would be considered a sexual sin and has spiritual consequences. The Bible warns us to "Flee sexual immorality. Every other sin that a person commits is outside the body, but the sexually immoral person sins against his own body" (1 Corinthians 6:18). Trusting God's plan for our lives is essential, rather than trying to take control ourselves. Remember, you are fearfully and wonderfully made (Psalm 139:14). You are loved by your Creator. Embrace who you are and trust in God's plan for your future.

• **Tara:** "You're judging me by telling me I shouldn't be trans and Jesus said, 'Do not judge.'"

Response: When discussing LGBTQ+ topics, some of your friends may reference Matthew 7:1 ("Do not judge so that you will not be judged"), advocating for love and acceptance of their chosen lifestyle. It's important to understand how to respond to this perspective. In Matthew chapters 5-7, Jesus criticized the scribes and Pharisees for their hypocritical behavior and misuse of the Old Testament. In Matthew 6:1-18, Jesus taught about not doing good deeds, praying, or fasting just to be seen by others and warned against holding a double standard. Instead, Jesus instructs us to "first take the log out of your own eye, and then you will see clearly to take the speck out of your brother's eye!" (Matthew 7:5). This means we should approach others' sin with love after acknowledging our own weaknesses.

Jesus was not saying we can never judge, but rather that our judgements should be fair and just. In Matthew 28, Jesus instructed His disciples to go and teach the lost, which involved recognizing who was saved and lost in the process.[30] Before sharing the gospel, we have to determine who is or isn't a Christian. Are they saved in Christ by having obeyed God's plan for salvation or do they not know Jesus yet? Jesus also told the Jews in John 7:24 to "judge with righteous judgment." This includes caring enough to help guide people away from sin, as stated in John 14:15, "If you love me, keep my commandments." From the previous scriptural references, we know that an LGBTQ+ lifestyle goes against God's commandments, which can jeopardize salvation. Loving others means having the desire to protect them from perishing in their sins. This love should motivate us to have heartfelt conversations when they embrace a lifestyle that God condemns. In Galatians 6:1, we are instructed to restore an individual caught in any wrongdoing with a spirit of gentleness, being aware of our own weakness to temptation. This means approaching others with humbleness instead of thinking we're superior. It also includes not ignoring someone who is heading down the wrong path. True love drives us to engage in these conversations.

Taking a Stand: Upholding Biblical Truth in a Changing World

So how do we navigate this new cultural movement to protect our purity? First, let's distance ourselves from activities that endorse the LGBTQ+ lifestyle. Unsubscribing from influencers and avoiding media or books that promote homosexuality and transgenderism might limit our entertainment choices, but it is absolutely necessary! We also have to love others enough to *gently* share the truth, restoring a sense of normalcy among teens and their desires. Most importantly, we must always stand up for the significance of the Cross. Isn't our Savior worth it? Let's adopt the courageous words of Esther, who said, "...and if I perish, I perish" (4:16) when she fought to save the Jewish people. Esther was willing to risk everything for God's purpose. Our true home is not of this world, and though we may face punishment and persecution for upholding the purity of the Gospel, our heavenly home will be worth it all.

It's Time for Reflection!

1. This week, take time to reflect on the new concepts you have been presented with during this chapter. Go back through the chapter to highlight and jot down talking points that you can use for future conversations on this subject. You will feel much more confident discussing this important topic if you've prepared your thoughts ahead of time.

2. Are there still things that you have questions about or don't seem to make sense? Write down those questions and ask a respected minister, spiritual mentor, or Bible class teacher to help you better understand these important concepts.

Chapter 10

Exploring Dating

♥ ♥ ♥ ♥ ♥ ♥ ♥ ♥ ♥ ♥ ♥ ♥ ♥ ♥ ♥

*"Mommy, there's one thing I know for sure about any man
I'm going to marry…He's gonna have at least one tattoo."*

When I encouraged my children to start thinking about the qualities of the man they want to marry, I never imagined tattoos would make it to the very top of the list. But in all fairness, my middle child has always viewed her daddy as her own personal superhero and he has tattoos, so I guess it makes sense. Even though my children are still relatively young, I believe it's important for them to start reflecting on the qualities they desire in a future spouse. Why is it so important to help guide them as they navigate preferences in the guys they date? Because, besides becoming a Christian yourself, who you choose to date and ultimately marry will have a profound spiritual impact on your life—more than anything else you do! It's a critical part of staying spiritually grounded throughout your life. If you haven't given much thought to this topic, I hope this chapter will provide you with a deeper understanding of why it's a crucial aspect in maintaining purity in your relationship with the Lord.

There's no doubt about it, the dating scene is tough for anyone these days. Dating relationships have become primarily digital so face-to-face interactions have become extremely awkward. Many guys are skipping the courting phase and jumping right into sex when they have the opportunity to be physically present with their girlfriends. I believe it's because they think it is the ultimate purpose of dating and relationships. Media and social influences encourage and glamorize the idea of being sexually active with your boyfriend. Engaging in sexual relationships has become a common and accepted part of growing up in our culture. Although culture teaches you that dating and sex are synonymous, this couldn't be further from the truth.

Have you ever taken the time to reflect on the true purpose of dating? When I was in my teens, dating was primarily about getting a free meal out with a cute guy and being able to call him your boyfriend. But is that what God intended for dating? Certainly not. The genuine purpose of dating is to get to know the man you're with, how he feels about himself, how he treats his family and others, and, most importantly, to identify how dedicated he is to the Lord.

Dating provides a glimpse into the traits of the man you want to be with—his personality, his quirks, and his habits, both good and bad. By dating, you're better able to answer questions like, "Can I live with his personality quirks forever or will they eventually drive me too crazy? Do our personalities work well together? Can I imagine living to the point of death with this person regardless of the difficulties and blessings that come our way?" Dating is also an opportunity to explore your future goals as a couple prior to marriage and to make sure they align. Does your future spouse desire to live near family or would he prefer to reside a distance from them? Does your future mate desire to have children or does he prefer a child-free marriage? How would he feel about you choosing to stay at home with your kids? What's your parenting style going to be like? Is he willing to follow God's plan for parenting? I want to take a moment now to encourage you to write down a list of questions you view as important in choosing a mate, then let a spiritual mentor in your congregation look them over and add to them for you. I promise you won't regret it!

An important goal in your dating relationship should be to discover whether the man you're with is capable of living out Ephesians 5:25-27 once you're married. This passage reads,

> "Husbands, love your wives, just as Christ also loved the church and gave Himself up for her, so that He might sanctify her, having cleansed her by the washing of water with the Word, that He might present to Himself the church in all her glory, having no spot or wrinkle or any such thing; but that she would be holy and blameless."

Girls, loving you like Christ loved the church takes tremendous work, sacrifice, and maturity. I'm not suggesting you should drop your boyfriend if he isn't willing to go all the way to the cross for you, but instead, consider whether he can even fulfill that command once you're married. There will be areas where you'll need to extend grace while he is maturing and striving to imitate those traits; you, too, will need that same level of grace. But, there are behaviors you can look for in the guys you date that will clue you in to whether they will eventually love you like Christ loved the church. Does he actively listen to your thoughts and feelings, and is he emotionally supportive? Does he display empathy and kindness to his friends and others he meets? Is he able to handle conflict in a constructive manner or does he routinely lash out in anger? Does he respect his mother or is his response toward her harsh and disrespectful? (Girls, how your boyfriend treats his mother speaks volumes about how he will respond to you after marriage!) Does he show commitment in relationships or in other areas of his life, or does he frequently rotate girlfriends and slack on other commitments? Does he respect you, or is he pushing the personal boundaries you've established at every turn? Keep in mind that a godly man will demonstrate love, honor, and respect towards you. He will value you as a woman worthy of dignity and honor by respecting your body. He will appreciate the inspired Word that provides guidance on maintaining sexual purity. He will take verses like 1 Thessalonians 4:3-6 to heart, which states,

> "For this is the will of God, your sanctification; that is, that you abstain from sexual immorality; that each of you know how to possess his own vessel in sanctification and honor, not in lustful passion, like the Gentiles who do not know God; and that no one violate the rights and take advantage of his brother or sister in the matter, because the Lord is the avenger in all these things, just as we also told you previously and solemnly warned you."

Navigating Modern Dating Challenges

Because we live in such a tech-driven world, many of you are getting a flawed perspective on how you are to be treated in dating relationships. Not long ago, I went out to eat with a large group of teenagers and within that group was a young dating couple. During the entire meal, the girl's boyfriend played video games on his phone while she stared at him intently. Occasionally, he'd look up at her, smile, and then return to his phone. Girls, if this happens to you, RUN! Run as fast as you possibly can from this type of relationship. You are in serious trouble if a guy in the dating phase of the relationship (when he should be totally infatuated with you) cannot separate from his device long enough to have a face-to-face conversation with you. This was a heart-sinking moment for me. It's just so sad that girls are starting to believe this is "normal" behavior.

Recently, a spiritual mentor shared with me about a conversation she had with her husband after he continuously engaged in technology during their lunch dates. "It's embarrassing to me when you're on your phone when we're out to eat. What are you telling other people about me? I am worth more than that!" Obviously, many guys are clueless in this area. In that same way, when you are out to eat or on a date, put your phone away (after the couple's selfie you really want to post on social media, of course)! It's disrespectful to the guy you are with to put technology above him when you're together. I promise everything on social media will still be there after that date is over!

Maintaining Purity in a Dating Relationship

We live in an age where more than 62 percent of Americans think it's okay for adults to have casual sexual relationships.[1] Media and culture play a significant role in promoting and portraying sex as cool on TV and social media, making it seem like a regular and accepted part of the teenage experience. By seventeen, 53 percent of girls will have already been in a sexual relationship.[2] In many of today's teen dating relationships, sex is increasingly used as a temporary substitute for genuine emotional needs, even though it does not deliver as promised. Relying on sexual activity to fulfill emotional needs can lead to depression, low self-esteem, and unsatisfying relationships both in the present and future. Besides that, did you know that a guy—especially one addicted to pornography—may not stay emotionally attached to you at all, even if he's having sex with you? He may use you for his own pleasure and drop you without any regret. Sadly, some girls feel pressured to participate in sexual activity just to be sure their boyfriends will stay with them. But what eventually happens when your attention is predominantly centered on what your boyfriend will do if you don't give yourself sexually to him? You begin compromising your body, heart, and soul. Listen, if a guy says, "I love you *when* you have sex with me" or "*because* you send naked pictures of yourself," rather than just "I love you," he is not suitable for dating, let alone marriage. Not only that but giving in to sexual temptation creates a performance-based dynamic where your acceptance is solely dependent on meeting his desires and expectations. You're not respected for who you are but for what you do. Your value and dignity are lost. Instead of providing happiness and fulfillment, having sex outside of God's intended design is filled with heartache, deception, pressure, and disappointment.

Some of you reading this chapter may think to yourself, "I'm in the clear. I've never crossed the line by engaging in sexual activity." But, how far is too far? Too often, we play the mental game of, "How much can I get away with and still be pure in God's eyes?" Is there a difference between "purity" and "virginity?" Is it possible to technically be a virgin while compromising your sexual purity through other means? Absolutely! While sexual abstinence before marriage is part of purity, God's expectations require more than just this aspect. Purity includes a lifestyle and an everyday mode of being. The true essence of purity goes back to the thoughts you dwell on, desires you act on, and actions that precede any physical intimacy. Too often when purity is addressed, it almost exclusively focuses on whether an individual has engaged in sexual activity, rather than considering if they have compromised any other aspect of their body or mind. Ephesians 5:5 reminds us that true purity involves avoiding all forms of sexual immorality or impurity, as they will keep us from inheriting eternal life.

Nurturing Purity: Establishing Boundaries in Dating Relationships

To protect your purity and make wise dating choices, let me encourage you to be extremely cautious about dating non-Christians. Remember, girls, guys are designed by God to be driven by what they see, physically. You'll find it difficult (although you can do it) to maintain sexual purity even while dating a Christian. But the chances of things not going too far with someone who is of this highly-sexualized, self-centered world are very slim. Not only that, if the purpose of dating is preparation for marriage, do you really want to be with someone who isn't spiritually focused? Don't you want to establish a foundation built on a shared commitment to God's Word while you grow together in your relationship with Him? Is a guy truly going to respect and assist you in maintaining your focus on Heaven if he doesn't share your values and faith? That's likely why 2 Corinthians 6:14 reminds us, "Do not be mismatched with unbelievers; for what do righteousness and lawlessness share together, or what does light have in common with darkness?" Obviously, dating isn't marriage, so it doesn't mean you can't teach the gospel to the man you're in a relationship with. However, reflect on verses like these before you get into a serious dating relationship with someone who isn't committed to loving and honoring God.

To maintain purity in your dating relationships, it's important to be proactive in developing boundaries ahead of time.

Coming from the girl who got the *All About Your Body* book when I was headed off to college, clearly my mom wasn't comfortable talking about sexual purity. If your parents were like mine, you're going to have to place appropriate boundaries on yourself! Here are some simple guidelines to help you maintain purity in your dating relationships:

❀ Pray with your boyfriend before you go out on a date—not just before you eat your meal. This will help you maintain the right mindset when you're together.

❀ Study the Bible together. There's nothing better than growing together in God's Word.

❀ Spend most of your time with your boyfriend in a group setting. Temptation will be less in these situations.

❀ If you're in a room together, leave the door open and don't lay down together. Generally, nothing good comes out of spending time alone in the bedroom behind closed doors with someone you are wildly attracted to.

❀ Keep kissing to a light peck. Remember, guys are more sexually driven. When you start passionately kissing, it can quickly evolve into much more.

Have an accountability partner you can turn to if you're feeling overwhelmed and struggling to make the right decisions in your dating relationship. You will find that a strong Christian sister who checks in with you regularly will be extremely helpful in keeping purity a priority in your dating relationships.

Embracing God's Design for Marriage

Why is it crucial to your spiritual health to protect your purity? Because you're preparing your heart for marriage. There are many lies presented about marriage in the culture we live in today that contradict God's design for marriage. Here's a few you may have heard:

- Love is love. Marry whomever you want.
- Only give as much as your spouse does in the marital relationship.
- God wants you to be happy. You deserve to be happy! If your personal happiness dissolves, so should your marriage.

Contrary to the messages conveyed by popular culture, God designed marriage to help you move into a closer relationship with Him as a couple. The scripture in Matthew 19 indicates that from the beginning God made the union between male and female. The two are "no longer two, but one flesh. Therefore, what God has joined together, no person is to separate" (Matthew 19:5-6). You'll find that the world builds relationships almost entirely on feelings and, as I'm sure you are already aware of, our emotions frequently change. What has feelings-based relationships resulted in? A divorce rate of 40 to 50 percent of first-time marriages.[3] This results from individuals elevating their own personal happiness over everything else in the relationship. When relationships are primarily focused on how *I feel* and *what I get out of the relationship*, they are filled with conflict and disappointment. If happiness is our primary goal, we'll get a divorce as soon as our personal happiness fades away. If our main objective is to receive love, we'll quickly end our relationship with our spouse as soon as they aren't attentive enough.[4] God's design for marriage is for something far greater than your temporary happiness on Earth. It's about holiness over happiness.

God uniquely designed marriage not only to make you happy, but to show His love and commitment to us. Marriage mirrors God's commitment with His people.[5] In Isaiah 54:5, it states, "For your husband is your Maker, Whose name is the LORD of armies; And your Redeemer is the Holy One of Israel, Who is called the God of all the earth." This means that God is like a loving spouse to us. When you get married, you're making a promise not just to your husband, but also to God. Even when you're mad at your spouse, remember that commitment you made to God. Christians don't give up on each other when our marriage gets tough. We extend grace and demonstrate loving-kindness just as God does for us. Love takes sacrifice and puts your spouse first, even before yourself. If you'll marry a Christian and maintain the right mindset by modeling God's love and commitment to His children, your marriage has the potential to be exactly what it was created to be—absolutely amazing!

God's Truths for Sexual Intimacy in Marriage

I'm uncertain what your experience has been, but it seems sex is often viewed in a negative light among Christians. We invest a significant amount of time into discussing all the reasons why you shouldn't engage in sex prior to marriage. But, I want you to understand the beauty of sexual intimacy as God designed it! We get a first glance of God's intention for sex in Genesis 2:24, when it emphasizes the unity and oneness achieved through the sexual union of a husband and wife. Proverbs 5:18-19 speaks of the pleasure and satisfaction experienced through physical intimacy in marriage: "Let your fountain be blessed, And rejoice in the wife of your youth. Like a loving doe and a

graceful mountain goat, Let her breasts satisfy you at all times; Be exhilarated always with her love." The Song of Solomon is an entire book dedicated to the beauty of love and sexual intimacy found between a husband and wife. In Song of Solomon 4:9-10, Solomon vows, "You have enchanted my heart, my sister, my bride; You have enchanted my heart with a single glance of your eyes, With a single strand of your necklace. How beautiful is your love, my sister, my bride! How much sweeter is your love than wine, And the fragrance of your oils than that of all kinds of balsam oils!"

If you participate in sexual intimacy in the way God designed it, it will be a beautiful and fulfilling experience. God designed physical intimacy in marriage to bond you together with your spouse. Through sexual intimacy, neurochemical changes occur in the brain that encourage emotional bonding among both individuals.[6] Oxytocin is often referred to as the "cuddle hormone" or "love hormone" because it does simply that—it creates a bond, trust, and generosity in us. Isn't it amazing how God designed the sexual relationship to strengthen and build intimacy in our marriages when we use it for its intended purpose?

Safeguarding Purity: Setting the Standard Now!

How can you prepare for purity in your relationships? First and foremost, don't compromise your standards! But how exactly can you keep yourself from a compromising situation? Decide ahead of time where your boundaries will be before finding yourself in a heated moment with the guy you're "in love with." I want to share the steps to physical intimacy so you can be prepared now on how far you're going to let yourself go before marriage.

1. Making eye contact with a guy you find attractive
2. Sharing in meaningful conversation
3. Giving each other a gentle hug
4. Holding hands
5. Hands on shoulders and hands on waist
6. A soft kiss on the cheek or lips
7. Open-mouthed passionate kissing
8. Intimate caressing while clothed
9. Exploring each other's body while naked
10. Sexual intercourse

(Adapted from Dannah Gresh, "And the Bride Wore White")[7]

Now that you know the steps, I want you to establish a clear boundary by circling the number where you plan to stop any form of physical contact.[8] As you consider your limit, remember—you should only go as far with your boyfriend as you would be comfortable doing in front of your father. Even if you're not in the presence of your earthly father, you're *always* in front of your Heavenly Father. And remember, God is not against physical intimacy. In fact, He loves it so much He put a covenant around it! He wants you to experience intimacy in a way that will bring closeness and strengthen your relationship with your husband, thus drawing you closer to Him. Keeping in mind that God doesn't want "even a hint of sexual immorality" in your relationship, would He be pleased with where you've stopped physical contact? If not, fix it. Predetermining this boundary will be a tremendous benefit to you when temptations arise. If you wait until the heat of the moment, you'll soon discover that "sin takes you further than you wanted to go, keeps you longer than you intended to stay, and costs you more than you intended to pay."[9] When emotions begin to escalate in your future dating relationships, reflect back to the limit you set and let it be the mental alarm that tells you, "I'm not compromising on purity."

Forgiving Self: The Path to Redemption

Some of you reading this chapter have already crossed the line of sexual impurity. You've gone too far in your dating relationships, or perhaps you've lived an "alternative" sexual lifestyle that is not acceptable to God. But guess what? So have so many others, including those in the church at Corinth. I'd like to refer to 1 Corinthians 6:9-11:

> "Or do you not know that the unrighteous will not inherit the kingdom of God? Do not be deceived; neither the sexually immoral, nor idolaters, nor adulterers, nor homosexuals, nor thieves, nor the greedy, nor those habitually drunk, nor verbal abusers, nor swindlers, will inherit the kingdom of God. Such were some of you;

but you were washed, but you were sanctified, but you were justified in the name of the Lord Jesus Christ and in the Spirit of our God."

The beauty of being a child of God is that He will make you whole again! Yet, forgiving yourself is one of the most difficult things you will do. I'll confess, it was one of the greatest mental battles I encountered during my early teen years. I believe these challenges arise because we buy into Satan's lies that we aren't deserving or worthy, or that our past mistakes are unforgivable, preventing our redemption. Don't believe the false messages Satan presents to you, girls. You are not hopeless! You can be redeemed! If you're a Christian who has stopped participating in the behaviors that don't align with the Lord and asked for forgiveness, God has already nailed that sin to the cross. God loves you! The blood of Jesus is powerful and will cleanse you of any sin you confess and turn from. He's willing to bring you back an infinite number of times if you have the right heart (Matthew 18:21-22). Maybe you're like me and have failed God in the past; let me plead with you to forgive yourself, get back up, and renew your walk with Christ. Now is the time to set out on the journey to redeem your sexual purity!

It's Time for Reflection!

This week, take time to discover what you want in your future spouse. Create a Top Ten list to keep for the future. Consider these areas for reflection:

1. The Inside Matters—Important Qualities in A Future Spouse:

What personality traits do you admire? Are you into humor, adventure, an easy-going personality, or someone serious? Think about important qualities like honesty, respect, compassion, and kindness. Which of these are important to you in the man you'll marry?

2. Planning Ahead—Future Goals for Marriage:

What dreams do you have for the future? Are they similar to what you'd want in a spouse? Consider where you'd like to live, if you want kids, and how you see each other's roles in marriage.

3. Faith and Family—Pursuing Spiritual Connections:

What spiritual attributes would you like in your spouse? Which of these qualities will he need to be the leader of your family? What religious beliefs are important to you for your future mate? Think about how someone's dedication to their convictions might impact your relationship.

4. The Ideal Husband—Going Beyond Looks:

Do you have preferences for how your spouse looks? Does the man of your dreams have an athletic build or slender physique? Short or long hair? Is he tall or short? Remember, though, appearances change over time—it's what's inside that matters most.[10]

Chapter 11

Addressing Recreational Drug and Alcohol Use

✔ ✔ ✔ ✔ ✔ ✔ ✔ ✔ ✔ ✔ ✔ ✔ ✔ ✔ ✔ ✔

"I destroy homes, tear families apart, take your children, and that's just the start. I'm more costly than diamonds, more costly than gold, the sorrow I bring is a sight to behold, and if you need me, remember I'm easily found. I live all around you, in schools and in town. I live with the rich, I live with the poor, I live down the street, and maybe next door. My power is awesome; try me you'll see, but if you do, you may never break free."[1]

As a teenager getting ready for adulthood, it's likely that even if you haven't been personally impacted by drugs, you've seen it affect someone you know, like a close friend or family member. Your teenage years open the door to a world filled with unlimited choices and experiences. We are told in 1 Timothy to "deny ungodliness and all worldly desires and to live sensibly, righteously, and in a godly manner" (2:12). Instead, many teens choose the path that promises exciting and new friendships, a feeling of belonging, and temporary enjoyment. New freedoms and independence in adolescence provide teens with the opportunity to try things like harmful substances. Drinking, vaping, and using drugs seem like a *normal* part of the teenage experience. As you consider whether or not to participate, you may begin having thoughts like, "I'm only gonna to do it once." But the reality is, even "one-time use" has the potential to set you up for a lifetime of heartache. In today's world, it's more realistic than ever that if you experiment with drugs or alcohol, it could kill you or someone else. Don't believe me?

Allow me to introduce you to Dawn Simmons, a mother whose life was forever changed by the impact of just one choice. Three children, full of hope, dreams, and a promising life, were taken in an instant. Dawn lost twenty-year-old Lindy, seventeen-year-old Christopher, and fifteen-year-old Kamryn when a drunk driver crashed into them. Shortly after her painful loss, Dawn wrote, "The emptiness of the house screams their absence every day. I never thought that I would miss having piles of laundry to fold. I never thought that I would miss having to stop at the store every day or a few times a day…I miss it all."[2] Even the routine chores now serve as a painful reminder to this family of lives taken too soon. "All of our hopes, dreams and family dynamics were gone," Dawn said. If you've ever experienced great loss, you can understand the absolute horror and pain this mother endures because someone thought they were just having a good time.[3]

Simah Herman is a young woman who fully understands the negative outcomes of a vaping addiction. As a teen who vaped every ten to fifteen minutes, what Simah thought was a harmless habit almost led to her death. At eighteen years old, Herman was hospitalized after she sat in her car, unable to breathe. "I just remember feeling like absolute…nothing. Like I just couldn't do anything," Herman said. "I couldn't drink water. I couldn't move. Like, I literally just wanted to crawl out of my skin."[4] Still unable to breathe after two days, Herman had to be put on a ventilator, and shortly afterward, a medically-induced coma caused by a strong inflammatory reaction to the vape product. Once she emerged from her coma, the first thing Simah did when she opened her eyes was to ask for a pen and paper since it was the only way she could communicate. On the paper, Simah wrote, "I want to start a no-vaping campaign."[5]

Ever wonder why some choices seem irresistible even when we know they lead to trouble? Picture this: the very things that offer a quick escape and brief moments of pleasure could actually create many more unexpected and unintended problems. In a world where scientific evidence highlights the negative effects of drug and alcohol use, one might think there wouldn't be such a temptation to use it. But, as long as there's sin in this world, substances that offer a temporary escape from problems will always be enticing. It probably doesn't come as a shock to you that alcohol tops the list among teen drug preferences, followed by marijuana use, and then nicotine vaping.[6] In this chapter, I'll share what the Christian teens I interviewed thought about using drugs and alcohol for fun, and why a lot of them choose not to do it. But for now, let's explore some of the most popular substances used by teenagers today so you'll understand a little more about how they affect your ability to live a radiant and redeemed life.

Navigating the Hazards of E-Cigarette Use: Unmasking Misconceptions and Realities

Since vaping has consistently become more popular and available to teens, you may have seen, heard, or even become one of more than 2.5 million middle and high school students across the United States using electronic cigarettes daily.[7] In speaking with teens, they've said, "vaping is everywhere…everyone is doing it." This might be because teenagers often have misunderstandings about vaping, such as:

- It's safer than smoking.
- My friends vape and they seem fine.
- I like all the fun flavors.
- It helps me relax and feel less anxious.
- I like the way it feels when I get a rush.[8]

Did you know that what many believe is a fun social activity can expose you to dangerous chemicals and addictive substances? Let me share a few facts about nicotine vaping you may not realize. Were you aware that 99 percent of electronic cigarettes sold in the US contain nicotine, the same highly addictive substance found in regular cigarettes?[9] When you vape, nicotine reaches your brain in as little as ten seconds and triggers a surge of dopamine. Even more alarming is that some vaping devices may contain as much nicotine as a pack of twenty regular cigarettes![10] Can you imagine the effect this would have on your body?!

Were you aware, too, that nicotine exposure changes the way your brain works, causing you to crave it more and become addicted? Many young people turn to vaping as a way to cope with stress or anxiety, but nicotine dependence only leads to additional stress on the brain and body. Nicotine use during adolescence can disrupt normal brain development by negatively affecting areas responsible for functions like attention, learning, mood, and impulse control.[11] E-cigarettes also contain harmful chemicals like formaldehyde, acrolein, and acetaldehyde, which are known to cause irreversible lung damage.[12] In addition, vaping aerosols can cause you to inhale toxic metal chemicals into your body. Although using e-cigarettes may seem like an appealing way to break free from boring routines, it is actually a habit that can lead to addiction, bringing lifelong physical and emotional consequences. Let Simah Herman's words be the voice of reason for you! Don't wait until you're sitting in a hospital bed, rehab center, or worse (meeting your Creator at the hands of a vape addiction) to stop using—now is the time!

The Allure and Impact of Cannabis Culture on Teens

With brightly-packaged candies advertising catchy flavors like "Mad Mango," "Loud Lemonade," and "Peach Dream," it's understandable that even Christian teens are drawn to marijuana-infused sweet treats. You probably know that edibles and vaping products are often advertised to teenagers on social media and video-sharing platforms online. They are designed to look appealing, secretive, and easy to use. How is the popularization of cannabis culture influencing your generation? A study conducted by Oregon Health & Science University revealed that marijuana abuse among teenagers in the United States has increased drastically—by about 245 percent—in a twenty year period![13]

While there is no doubt that a mix of factors contributes to this rise, it may be partly due to the gradual increase in the amount of tetrahydrocannabinol (THC) in marijuana over the past few decades.[14] It only makes sense that if you're taking in higher THC levels, then your risk for abuse and addiction will also increase. What social media influencers, celebrities, and your peers aren't so eager to share with you are the short- and long-term effects of using this drug.

Let me break down the scientific principles behind how marijuana impacts your body in case you aren't familiar. When someone consumes marijuana, the active compound, THC, quickly enters the bloodstream and is then transferred to the brain and various organs. Generally, these effects become noticeable within just thirty minutes to an hour. It's important to recognize that marijuana use can have negative consequences. These include challenges in thinking and problem solving, memory and learning difficulties, decreased coordination, struggles with attention, and disruptions in school and social life.[15] As a result, consistent or heavy marijuana use is known to have permanent effects on brain development. In higher doses, it can even induce impaired memory, hallucinations, and delusions.[16] Marijuana use has been associated with a range of mental health problems such as depression, anxiety, and suicidal thoughts among teens.[17]

Consequences of Drinking: The Risks & Impact on Families

Since over 60 percent of teenagers in the United States report drinking alcohol by the time they leave high school, it's a drug that absolutely must be discussed.[18] While underage drinking continues to remain a fun activity for teens, promising increased happiness and satisfaction, the actual consequences of using couldn't be further from its perception. In fact, did you realize that it contributes to the deaths of thousands of youth under age twenty-one in the United States each year? This includes:

- 1,573 from motor vehicle crashes
- 1,121 from homicides
- 190 from alcohol overdose, falls, burns, and drowning
- 718 from suicides[19]

In addition, were you aware that excessive alcohol use is a *leading preventable cause of death* in the United States?![20] Beyond the risk of death, drinking alcohol increases the likelihood of developing liver disease, heart disease, depression, stroke, and stomach bleeding, and various cancers.[21] Drinking alcohol during your teenage years can also disrupt normal adolescent brain development.[22] Is this truly an activity that aligns with Christian values? Proverbs 20:1 tells us that "wine is a mocker, intoxicating drink a brawler, and whoever is intoxicated by it is not wise." The Bible continues its message in Proverbs 23:31, cautioning not to "look on the wine when it is red, when it sparkles in the cup, when it goes down smoothly." But why such a warning? Exploring further into verse 32 we discover that this is the moment that it "bites like a serpent and stings like a viper."

Nothing good comes from a drug that interferes with your ability to think critically and make wise choices. If you find yourself justifying drinking by thinking you'll stop when you're a little older, be careful! That's not how addiction works. F. Scott Fitzgerald once said, "First you take a drink, then the drink takes a drink, then the drink takes you."[23] You may think you're just experimenting but you could quickly end up on a downward spiral of dependency. It's not worth the long-term cost; the only way to prevent a substance abuse problem is to never pick up the bottle in the first place. Don't allow yourself to be fooled by Satan as Eve was, with one tempting bite!

Substance Use: From A Biblical Perspective

In speaking with Christian teens about how they escaped the temptation to use recreational drugs and alcohol, the overwhelming response was choosing friends who shared their same values (another shout out for building Christian friendships!) and understanding the health risks. Only a few could identify any logical reasoning from God's Word as to why we shouldn't engage in these activities. I want to provide you with some reasons from a biblical perspective as to why you should avoid using drugs and alcohol purely for enjoyment.

Throughout history, God established laws for His people to follow that were meant to help and take care of them. In the Old Testament this became clear with the introduction of the Ten Commandments. God provided a set of rules prohibiting things like murder, lying, or stealing—actions that are morally upright and beneficial to both ourselves and others. God still requires obedience by Christians today—obeying your parents (Ephesians 6:1), worshiping on the first day of the week (1 Corinthians 16:2), treating others with love and respect (Romans 12:10), and avoiding sinful behaviors (Colossians 3:5). Why would God impose all these rules on us? Is He trying to set us up for failure or take away all our fun? No, exactly the opposite! These guidelines are designed to enrich and protect our lives.

Each of God's commandments has a specific purpose and intention behind it, which ultimately guides us to a more fulfilling life. A similar principle applies when we consider using drugs and alcohol. One of these fundamental principles is being sober minded, which simply means having a clear and rational state of mind. To focus on spiritual things, the Bible commands repeatedly that we must be sober minded (Galatians 5:21, 1 Thessalonians 5:6, 1 Peter 1:13). In 1 Peter 5:8, God urges us, "Be of sober spirit, be on the alert. Your adversary, the devil, prowls around like a roaring lion, seeking someone to devour." In this scripture, God is encouraging us to be sober minded so that we can resist the temptation of sin and to protect us from our own poor decisions. We know drugs impair judgment and cloud reasoning; logically, then, we wouldn't want to consume a substance that would compromise our abilities to make sound and reasonable decisions.

Another biblical reason to avoid drugs and alcohol comes from the understanding that our bodies are not our own alone;

instead, they are a valuable gift from God. In 1 Corinthians 3:16-17, we are told, "Do you not know that you are a temple of God and that the Spirit of God dwells in you? If anyone destroys the temple of God, God will destroy that person; for the temple of God is holy, and that is what you are." Part of being pure and holy includes taking care of the body God gave us. This idea is further discussed in Romans 12:1, where Paul urges Christians to present their bodies as a living sacrifice, holy and pleasing to God, as an act of worship. As Christians, embracing purity involves cherishing and protecting the precious bodies God has given to us.

Daniel is an excellent example of someone who took extraordinary caution to ensure he was living a faithful life before God. When he faced Babylonian captivity, Daniel was offered the king's diet of royal food and wines, but he chose to abstain to set himself apart and honor the Lord (Daniel 1:8-16). His example shows us the importance of living a lifestyle that is distinct from the world, avoiding drugs that impair your judgment, and striving for purity and righteousness before God. So, be like Daniel—stay sober-minded and set yourself apart from the world's temptations, living in holiness and purity.

But God Created It

Some teens try to justify their use of alcohol, marijuana, or nicotine because the substances in these products were created by God. But think about this: God also created the castor bean plant, one of the most poisonous plants in the world because of its deadly substance, ricin, found within its seed. No one argues to eat or smoke this because "God made it." My point is, God made everything for a reason—for example, nicotine is meant to protect plants, not to be consumed. Humans are the ones who try to use things in nature in ways God didn't intend, which often leads to painful long-term consequences.

The reason behind the use of any drug matters. There are times when medicines, either found in nature or refined in a lab, may be needed to help with mental or physical problems. But, there's a significant difference between using drugs for purposes of medical treatment or simply for fun. When people use drugs like marijuana, the part of the cannabis plant consumed contains the highest levels of THC. This part of the plant contains mind-altering effects. It's not the portion of the plant used for medical conditions like epilepsy, multiple sclerosis, Alzheimer's, and fibromyalgia.[24] Once again, it might be a good time to do some self-reflection if you're feeling the need to rationalize having a "good time" with friends.

"You knew this would happen, many times you were told, but you challenged my power, and chose to be bold. You could have said no, and just walked away, if you could live that day over, now what would you say? I'll be your master; you will be my slave, I'll even go with you, when you go to your grave. Now that you have met me, what will you do? Will you try me or not? It's all up to you."[25]

What will your choice be? I hope you'll make the decision to walk away!

It's Time for Reflection!

1. This week, I want you to reflect on how your personal involvement with drug or alcohol use or indifference towards others using it has impacted your spiritual walk. In what ways, if any, has it caused you to conform to the world?

2. How do you believe society views the recreational use of substances and how do you think it impacts your influence and ability to encourage others to live righteously before God?

3. Grab a highlighter and highlight the negative consequences of engaging in these behaviors listed in the chapter.

4. Jot down at least three scriptures about the importance of protecting the body God blessed you with. Then, seek His guidance through prayer and studying scripture to help you walk in a way that would be pleasing to Him. If you're in a spot where you don't feel like you can break the habit on your own, seek help! Find a spiritual mentor who can help you stop this addictive habit before you suffer with the long-term effects of its use. Your family, your church, and your Creator love you and will walk with you through this. Find the resources you need to break the habit. The results could impact you for a lifetime.

Chapter 12

Choosing Wisely: The Power of Your Words

✔ ✔ ✔ ✔ ✔ ✔ ✔ ✔ ✔ ✔ ✔ ✔ ✔ ✔ ✔ ✔ ✔

When my twelve-year-old daughter placed her order during a recent family dinner at Jason's Deli, she requested a BLT with no lettuce or tomato, and no bun. When the waitress arrived delivering an entire plate of *just* bacon to her, she was utterly shocked and appalled! "Mama, they forgot my whole burger!" Poor Brooke thought a BLT included a hamburger patty, too, but her words got her exactly what she asked for. Thankfully, that misuse of words only cost her a little bit of frustration (and some good laughs by her parents) that night.

But, words are powerful, aren't they? Think about it. God created the entire universe and everything in it by simply speaking it into existence (Hebrews 11:3)! Of course, the power of our words isn't supernatural like God's, but our words still have a significant impact on those around us. In Proverbs 18:21, we're told, "Death and life are in the power of the tongue, and those who love it will eat its fruit." Our words have the power to encourage and uplift others, and to bring others into a closer relationship with our Creator. Recently, while I was on a flight, I observed another passenger compliment the necklace of the stranger near her, and it was remarkable how this individual willingly opened up to her afterward. Who knew that a simple compliment could open a door of conversation (and even better, give you the ability to share your faith)? On the flip side, our words also can be very dangerous by hurting relationships and damaging the self-image of our friends and family. If you've ever been intentionally excluded, repeatedly made fun of, or told you weren't good enough, you know how hurtful words can be.

As we begin this chapter, consider the different ways you use language, both the thoughts in mind (your inner voice) and the words you speak. What impact do your words have on others? Are you using your speech to help teach your friends about Jesus, or are you more likely to use it to tear others down? Do you find yourself wrapped in negative thoughts about others, or is it your habit to think positively instead? It takes but a split second to utter your words, but the effects (whether good or bad) can have a lasting impact. Think about how you can be more respectful of others by avoiding hurtful comments, spreading rumors, and using profanities and other offensive language. Instead, focus on the opportunities you have to express thankfulness to God, teach and encourage others, and build Christian relationships through the words you express as we strive for purity in this area of our daily life.

Beyond Sticks and Stones: Examining the Impact of Our Speech

We've all heard the saying, "Sticks and stones may break my bones, but words will never hurt me!" I'm not sure about you, but I don't think there's ever been a bigger lie told! If you've been made fun of for your looks, teased about being ugly or fat, or told you can't be a part of "the friend group," you understand just how inaccurate this statement is. It seems almost natural for us to use our words to belittle, damage, and destroy others. To be honest, a major part of our problem is that we dwell on every negative comment or action towards us. We allow these negative thoughts to take control of our mind and begin to shape who we are and how we respond to others. Chances are you've heard the statement, "Hurt people hurt people."[1] Isn't that just like us? We let negative thoughts about others run wild in our mind and begin to take over, which results in using our words to hurt others. Proverbs 11:9 reminds us, "With his mouth the godless person destroys his neighbor." Can we truly be living for Christ if we use our speech to purposely destroy the lives of others?

Connected to insults is our involvement in gossip, which includes intentionally spreading rumors about others. Truthfully, gossip seems to be a struggle for every human on this planet! Why is it such a challenge for us? Again, I'd connect it to the speech that begins to grow in our minds first. Sadly, gossip can destroy people, relationships, and even entire churches. Gossip is a lot like glitter—you can never truly clean it all up. It has lasting negative effects, and you keep finding specks of it despite cleaning efforts.

Much like wood is to a fire, a person who stirs up conflict through gossip and spreading rumors causes hurt feelings and destroys relationships. In Proverbs 26:20, this scripture reads, "For lack of wood the fire goes out, and where there is no gossiper, quarreling quiets down." This passage uses the metaphor of a fire to illustrate the idea that without fuel (represented by the wood) a fire would die out. Very similarly, when there's no one engaging in gossip, it, too, will cease. This scripture is a great reminder that we have control over whether we'll stop the gossip. Moving forward into verses 21-22, the Bible says, "Like charcoal to hot embers and wood to fire, so is a contentious person to kindle strife. The words of a gossiper are like dainty morsels, and they go down into the innermost parts of the body." In these verses, the fire metaphor is used to compare the whisperer to the wood that ignites the fire.

David had good reason to ask God in Psalms 141:3-4 to, "Set a guard, LORD, over my mouth; Keep watch over the door of my lips. Do not incline my heart to any evil thing, to practice deeds of wickedness with people who do wrong; And may I not taste their delicacies." Choosing your words carefully is not easy to do, but it can totally be done! Personally, I find it helpful to remember and use the acronym THINK when I'm communicating with or about others. Before speaking, ask yourself these questions: Is it True? Is it Helpful? Is it Inspiring? Is it Necessary? Is it Kind?[2] We need determination that the way we communicate with and about others is going to be different, or no one is going to believe we are a Christian.

Our Speech: A Window to Our Hearts

When you make the commitment to become a Christian by putting on Christ in baptism (Galatians 3:27), your speech should begin to change, too, and you should start using pure, wholesome, and praiseworthy language. Does this sound like you or your Christian friends? Instead of trying to live a righteous life before God, many people push the limits by living as close to the edge of sin as possible, while still attempting to identify as a Christian. Maybe you have friends like this, who use "almost" every profanity they can get away with (if not the actual curse words themselves) and have little to no respect for God's name. Why do we straddle the fence with the language we use? Ephesians 4:29 encourages us, "let no unwholesome word come out of your mouth." Again, in Colossians 3:8, we are also told to "rid yourselves of all of them: anger, wrath, malice, slander, and obscene speech from your mouth." In our pursuit of purity, we should speak with grace and kindness, using wisdom and respect in our conversations with others (Colossians 4:6). If you find yourself dwelling on negative, unwholesome talk, interrupt that thought pattern by reflecting on verses like this instead. Don't see how close you get to sin before sinning. Remember, Satan owns the fence. Don't straddle it!

Have you ever considered that your speech is an overflow of your heart? Our words demonstrate what we value most—whether it is the things of this world or of God. This is why your media, music, and friendship choices are so impactful on your life. If you choose wisely in these areas, it will limit the negative influences that affect your thoughts and heart. Matthew 15:18 teaches us that "the things that come out of the mouth come from the heart, and those things defile the person."

Can you see now how important it is to interrupt those negative thought patterns by dwelling on the positive instead? You have power and control over what you allow to influence your thoughts and speech. A heart shaped by the Word of God should guide you in choosing the right words, knowing when to speak, and recognizing when silence is best. James 1:26 says, "If anyone thinks himself to be religious, yet does not bridle his tongue but deceives his own heart, this person's religion is worthless." Two of my daughters take horseback riding lessons—the bridle is an important part of this process. The bridle helps the rider guide and control the horse's steps. In this same way, James is saying here that your heart should help you bridle your tongue. You need to develop enough self-control to change your thoughts and the words that come out of your mouth. If I haven't emphasized this enough yet, our words are so powerful! They can break us to the core or empower us to become stronger individuals. I hope you are working daily to use words that build others up instead of tearing them down.

Transforming Lives Through the Power of Your Words

Have you ever had a teacher, coach, or perhaps a spiritual mentor say something positive about you? In what ways did it influence your life? When I was in college, a minister I highly respected spoke positively about my character from the pulpit. It motivated me to aspire to do and be more for Christ. If you've had a similar experience, you understand the power genuine praise has to help you stay motivated as you walk on your spiritual journey. Let's spend some time now focusing on the ways in which you can use your speech in a positive way! Here are some practical strategies to consider:

Uplifting Others through Words of Encouragement:

❀ Look for opportunities to offer genuine compliments and praise, and to recognize the achievements of others. If your friend led her first girls' devotional, praise her for having the courage to do that! If your classmate just won an essay contest, congratulate them on their achievement. Recognize the strengths of others and look for practical ways to encourage them.

❀ "Anxiety in a person's heart weighs it down, but a good word makes it glad." Proverbs 12:25

Expressing Thankfulness in Your Words:

❀ Have a heart of gratitude! Use your speech to express thankfulness to your parents, teachers, and others around you who have an ongoing impact on your life. Consider doing a daily gratitude journal. Appreciate the "simple" things like air conditioning, good health, a warm bed at night—all the things God has blessed you with each day! It'll help you maintain a positive attitude and a grateful heart.

✸ "Rejoice always, pray without ceasing, in everything give thanks; for this is the will of God for you in Christ Jesus." 1 Thessalonians 5:16-18

Building Christian Friendships through Our Speech:

✸ Use your words to start building relationships with other Christians. These individuals will encourage you, guide you, hold you accountable, and help strengthen your faith. You're going to need them as you journey toward Heaven.

✸ "A friend loves at all times, and a brother is born for adversity." Proverbs 17:17

Using Our Words to Take Action:

✸ Equally as important as avoiding gossip yourself, take a stand and do something when you hear others gossiping. A youth minister visiting my church recently shared how one of his old classmates reached out to him as an adult and said that he had forgiven him for doing nothing when their peers were saying mean, hurtful things to him in school. *It's wrong when we're bystanders and do nothing, too!*

✸ "Two are better than one because they have a good return for their labor; for if either of them falls, the one will lift up his companion. But woe to the one who falls when there is not another to lift him up! Furthermore, if two lie down together they keep warm, but how can one be warm alone? And if one can overpower him who is alone, two can resist him. A cord of three strands is not quickly torn apart." Ecclesiastes 4:9-12

Influential Words—Sharing the Message of Jesus:

❀ Take every opportunity you have to use your words to influence others for Jesus. Our entire mission in life should revolve around saving souls for Christ. Church should especially be a place where your peers feel the most welcomed and encouraged to be a part of the group. We should be going out of our way to make every visitor who walks into our doors feel accepted and welcomed. We should be proactively seeking these visitors to help them develop a relationship with Christ. Sister-in-Christ Becky Blackmon once said, "What a travesty if we walked into Heaven alone." I couldn't agree more! Pray for opportunities to bring others to Christ. God will send someone to you who needs you. Go out to eat with them. Take them for coffee, shoot basketball, go on a walk or to the mall together, or just listen as they share their story.

❀ "And He said to them, 'Go into all the world and preach the gospel to all creation." Mark 16:15

Want to live a radiant and redeemed life? Take control of the language you speak, both in your mind and through your words. Dwell on the positive. Communicate in ways that will encourage and build up others. Be a source of inspiration to your peers by the way in which you praise and recognize the achievements of your friends. Let your speech motivate those around you to walk more closely with Jesus. Your words have amazing power! Use them in a way that will give glory to God.

It's Time for Reflection!

1. This week, take an inventory on your use of words. Does your speech promote love and kindness, or does it tend to be critical and negative? Are you using your words to encourage and support those around you, or do you often find yourself tearing others down by criticizing or gossiping? Are you using your speech to engage in conversations with those who don't know Jesus to help bring them to Christ?

2. How could you work on improving the way you communicate with others in your day-to-day life?

3. Identify at least three practical ways you could better use your words and pray that God will help you as you pursue purity in this area.

Chapter 13

Pursuing the Priceless Pearl

♥ ♥ ♥ ♥ ♥ ♥ ♥ ♥ ♥ ♥ ♥ ♥ ♥ ♥ ♥ ♥ ♥

"And you will seek Me and find Me when
you search for Me with all your heart."
~ Jeremiah 29:13

As I begin this final chapter on rediscovering purity through the lens of our Creator, Jeremiah 29:13 is the perfect verse to focus on. Our entire purpose in life should be to seek, know, and follow the commandments of our Lord. Why is this such a crucial aspect of being a follower of Christ? Because our eternity is at stake! In Matthew 13, Jesus uses a parable to demonstrate just how valuable it is to pursue the kingdom of Heaven. "Again, the kingdom of heaven is like a merchant seeking fine pearls, and upon finding one pearl of great value, he went and sold everything that he had and bought it" (Matthew 13:45-46). To appreciate the beauty of this verse, it's helpful to understand how natural pearls are created. Pearls start when something foreign gets inside of an oyster, making it irritated. The oyster responds by covering it, like the way a scab or Band-Aid protects a wound. The only difference is that an oyster will continue working on that pearl even after the first layers are down, which ultimately transforms it from something ugly into a beautiful and elegant gemstone.

Were you aware of these facts about pearls?

- Pearls are the only gemstone created inside a living creature.
- Only 1 percent of pearls in stores are true natural pearls; others are cultured.
- Natural pearls are among the rarest jewels in the world.
- On average, less than one in every 10,000 wild oysters contains pearls.
- The most expensive pearl is valued at over 100 million dollars.[1]
- Although natural pearls are similar in appearance, no two are exactly the same.

In our modern world, we don't fully appreciate the value of pearls because we're surrounded by a culture that produces them. In the early 1900's, prior to the creation of cultured pearls, natural pearls were so rare and expensive only the socially elite or very wealthy had them.[2] In Jesus' time, people understood their worth. In those days, most pearls were brought up by divers who would open hundreds or even thousands of oysters to find even one pearl. "So rare was the valuable pearl that often a man did have to sell all that he had—his land, his livestock, his servants, his home—to have enough to buy just one pearl of great price."[3] Will you let Jesus use your spiritual "irritants and imperfections" to bring about the pearl of great price in your life?

Living a Transformed Life: Trading in the Counterfeit Pearls

I don't know about you, but I've often found myself settling for counterfeit pearls. It's the very reason I chose to write this book. My goal is to help you overcome so many of the struggles I faced as a teen. Why do we so frequently find ourselves drawn to the counterfeit pearls in life? At first glance, imitation pearls appear almost identical to the real ones. But, in reality, fake pearls are very similar to a knockoff necklace. At first, counterfeit pearls are well-polished and glisten in the sun. But it doesn't take long until the finish wears off and starts to leave a mark around your neck.

Maybe your counterfeit pearls look something like this:

• Determining your self-worth based on the number of likes and shares you get on social media instead of finding value in being a daughter of the King.

• Being in a relationship with someone who uses you only for what he wants instead of being pleasing to God.

• Choosing to wear clothes that make you *feel* beautiful regardless of whether it glorifies God.

• Choosing inappropriate books, movies, and other forms of entertainment, or giving into the temptation of using offensive words, instead of choosing the narrow path that leads to eternal life.

There are times in every Christian's life when we substitute fake pearls for the pearl of great price. It's the times when I tell myself, "God wants me to be happy," so I substitute happiness in whatever way I find pleasurable instead of finding peace and contentment in being a child of God. Can you relate to any of these? Are you chasing after the empty pleasures of this world? Don't worry, you are not alone. God's own people struggled with this very same thing. His chosen ones, the Israelites, turned back to life of idolatry soon after He'd delivered them from the hands of Pharaoh, led them across the Red Sea, and made them ready to enter the Promised Land. Why? Their hearts turned back to Egypt (Acts 7:39-40). Although many Israelites initially believed and were faithful to God, they very quickly turned back to pagan worship.

We can be just like that, too—the times when we care

more about what our friends think than God, when we fall to peer pressure, or when we are more concerned about our own personal happiness over holiness. Remember, the Bible tells us that if we're not willing to give up everything for God, we cannot be His disciple (Luke 14:33). God's desire is to have all of you! And the truth is, if you were in His place, you would want that, too. Imagine if your best friend, boyfriend, mother, or father only wanted a relationship with you when it was convenient for them. You would feel neglected, disrespected, and unloved. Are you starting to get a glimpse of how God might feel based on how we treat Him? He wants you to give up all those counterfeit pearls to be fully devoted to Him.

In the book of Matthew, we are given the first and greatest commandment, "to love the Lord your God with all your heart, and with all your soul, and with all your mind" (22:37-38). Too often, though, our desire is to look just like the world while still claiming Christianity. It's obvious in the media we choose, the way we dress, the friendships we maintain, and our tolerance for the lifestyles God clearly condemns. But, our obedience to God is not cafeteria style—we can't take what we want and opt out of the rest.[4] If we've truly surrendered our hearts to God, we won't try to justify things like:

- Consuming media that repeatedly blasphemes the name of God (Leviticus 19:12; Matthew 6:9)
- Having sex before marriage (1 Corinthians 6:18-20; 1 Thessalonians 4:3-5)
- Changing the way God created men and women with their unique gender identities (Mark 10:6; Genesis 5:2)
- Participating in social drinking and recreational drug use (1 Peter 5:8; Proverbs 20:1)

- Attempting to find every loophole around following God's plan for salvation (Mark 16:16; Luke 13:3; Romans 10:9; Acts 22:16; Revelation 2:10)
- Treating our spiritual life like it's simply a check-the-box opportunity (Matthew 22:37-38; Revelation 3:16; James 2:17; Colossians 3:23-24)

Are you truly striving to be transformed into God's image or are you attempting to get Him to conform to yours? Instead of following what's popular in culture, our mindset should be, "How can I be more pleasing to God"? With every action we take, we should ask, "Can I give glory to God by participating in this?" By doing so, it will change the way we respond to purity! Contrary to pop culture and what your social media influencers say, obedience to God is the only way you'll find true happiness and fulfillment. If you'll let His Word guide you, it won't be such a struggle to know where to go to college, who to marry, what activities are acceptable, and what your plans for life should be.

Pursuing Purity: He is Worth it All

The saddest day of my life was the day my mom shared with me (while she was alone in the hospital during COVID) that she no longer wanted to endure the fight against cancer. After eight years of chemotherapy, radiation, and brain surgeries, she was ready to go to her eternal home. Although those last weeks of her life were heart-wrenching and painful, they were nothing compared to what our Saviour experienced on the Cross. You see, while my mom was in hospice care, we met her every need. We sang to her, prayed with her, and ensured her medication made her as comfortable as possible. She had a group of supporters rallying around her. But what Jesus endured leading up to and during His crucifixion on the cross was far more excruciating. Even worse, He didn't have a following of supporters encouraging Him—only mockers. Jesus experienced such sorrow in the Garden of Gethsemane that He begged God to "let this cup pass from me" (Matthew 26:39). The human side of Him didn't want to go through the physical pain and anguish He knew He was going to go through for you and me. And although Jesus went through tremendous suffering for us, most of us are so wrapped up in our own personal pleasures and desires that we aren't even willing to make the smallest of sacrifices to pursue purity in our relationship with Him. We aren't willing to stand up when it's uncomfortable or stand out when it's needed.

What will it take for you and me to reclaim purity again? Being a daughter of the King is the greatest, most fulfilling calling we'll experience, but surrendering to Him will be the key to our success. God wants all of you—every single bit! And so I ask, are you committed to obeying Him regardless of whether it makes you feel weird, awkward, uncool, or different from your friends (maybe even the Christian ones)? Are you ready to give up everything that stops you from pursuing purity in God's Kingdom? I hope so! Let's unite together as we rediscover purity and begin embracing a Radiant and Redeemed life!

It's Time for Reflection!

1. As you reflect on our journey of rediscovering purity over these last thirteen chapters, take a moment to consider the "fake pearls" in your life. Every one of our counterfeit pearls comes with a price tag that will leave you feeling empty and worthless. Search deep in your heart and identify the fake pearls you still need to give up to pursue the priceless pearl. What's holding you back and robbing you of your purity with Christ? Remember, if you aren't living a pure and righteous life, you aren't fulfilling God's plan for you. God wants you to trade in all the fake pearls in your life in order to pursue purity in your relationship with Christ. Until you let go of all the counterfeit pearls, you'll never truly grasp the fullness and goodness of God's blessings.[5]

2. Take this time to journal about the areas of life you want to improve. Pray about it every day this week! Never give up seeking that pearl of great price! It may cost us everything, but won't it be worth it in the end?

About the Author

Kate lives in Valdosta, Georgia, with her husband, Brian, and their three daughters. She finds great joy in teaching Bible classes and speaking at women's events. Kate holds a Bachelor's Degree in Criminal Justice from Faulkner University and a Master's in Social Work from Valdosta State University. As a Licensed Master Social Worker and Trust Based Relational Intervention® practitioner, she has dedicated her career to helping children and families involved with the Department of Families and Children Services. Kate's roles have included therapist, foster care supervisor, assessor, and educator. Currently, her primary focus is being a mom, which she believes is her greatest calling.

Endnotes

Chapter 1

1 "Purity Definition & Meaning." n.d. Dictionary.com. Accessed January 26, 2023. https://www.dictionary.com/browse/purity.

2 "World Population Clock: 8 Billion People (LIVE, 2022)." n.d. Worldometer. Accessed November 28, 2022. https://www.worldometers.info/world-population/.

Chapter 2

1 Jackson, Kevin. 2022. "Living Christian on X: "In Mark 2, Jesus healed a paralyzed man because of his friends' faith. This is why your circle matters." X.com. https://twitter.com/livechristian1/status/1581007183277219840?lang=en.

2 Gipford, Erin. 2015. "Confidence is Silent, Insecurities are Loud!" Jane Curnow. https://janecurnow.com/2015/04/03/confidence-is-silent-insecurities-are-loud/.

3 Lenae, Ashton. 2013. "susie & sally." The Girl Who Loved to Write. https://thegirlwholovedtowrite.com/2013/05/susie-sally/.

Chapter 3

1 Morin, Amy. 2022. "How the Media Can Harm Your Teen's Body Image." Verywell Family. https://www.verywellfamily.com/media-and-teens-body-image-2611245 (Accessed 20 November 2022); "Media's Effect On Girls: Body Image And Gender Identity | MediaWise.org." 2009. National Institute on Media and the Family. https://www.mediafamily.org/facts/facts_mediaeffect.shtml. (Accessed 20 November 2022).

2 Gill, Rosalind. 2020. Changing the perfect picture: Smartphones, social media and appearance pressures,, 54. https://www.city.ac.uk/__data/assets/pdf_file/0005/597209/Parliament-Report-web.pdf. (Accessed 1 November 2022).

3 Ibid

4 "Understanding Body Dysmorphic Disorder (BDD)." 2022. Anxiety and Depression Association of America, ADAA. https://adaa.org/understanding-anxiety/body-dysmorphic-disorder. (Accessed 24 November 2022).

5 Melton, Glennon D., dir. 2013. Lessons from the Mental Hospital. https://www.youtube.com/watch?v=NHHPNMIK-fY&t=531. (Accessed 1 November 2022).

6 Beals, Sarah. 2019. "The Real You. A lesson in identity for teen girls youth groups." Joy-Filled Days. https://joyfilleddays.com/the-real-you-a-lesson-in-identity-for-teen-girls-youth-groups/. (Accessed 27 November 2022).

7 Ibid.

8 Allen, Jennie. 2020. Get Out of Your Head: Stopping the Spiral of Toxic Thoughts. N.p10.: Crown Publishing Group, 10.

9 Ibid, 5.

10 Sasson, Remez. n.d. "How Many Thoughts Does Your Mind Think in One Hour?" Success Consciousness. (Accessed November 27, 2022). https://www.successconsciousness.com/blog/inner-peace/how-many-thoughts-does-your-mind-think-in-one-hour/; "Brain Facts - Healthy Brains by Cleveland Clinic." n.d. HealthyBrains.org. (Accessed November 27, 2022). https://healthybrains.org/brain-facts/.

11 Hope, Faith. 2012. "80 % of Thoughts Are Negative...95 % are repetitive – The Miracle Zone." The Miracle Zone. https://faithhope-andpsychology.wordpress.com/2012/03/02/80-of-thoughts-are-nega-tive-95-are-repetitive/. (Accessed 21 November 2022).

12 "How to Turn Around Your Negative Thinking." 2019. Cleveland Clinic. https://health.clevelandclinic.org/turn-around-negative-thinking/. (Accessed 15 November 2022).

13 Ridsdel, Joan. 2023. "10 Common Negative Thinking Patterns and 5 Steps for Change." The Family Centre. https://www.familycentre.org/news/post/10-common-negative-thinking-patterns-and-5-steps-for-change.

14 Nicole, Danielle. n.d. S-O-S, Negative Self-Talk Stopping Technique. https://www.pinterest.com/pin/68740356580/. (Accessed 27 November 2022).

Chapter 4

1 Whitaker, Anita. 2002. Straddling the Fence. N.p.30: Publishing Designs, Incorporated.

2 Hawkes, Keith. 2022. "The Fallout Movie Review for Parents." Parent Previews. https://parentpreviews.com/movie-reviews/the-fallout#content-details. Accessed December 15, 2022.

3 Camacho, Melissa. 2023. "Pretty Little Liars: Original Sin TV Review." Common Sense Media. https://www.commonsensemedia.org/tv-reviews/pretty-little-liars-original-sin.

4 Ashby, Emily. 2022. "Outer Banks TV Review." Common Sense Media. https://www.commonsensemedia.org/tv-reviews/outer-banks. Accessed December 15, 2022.

5 "CLASSIFICATION AND RATING RULES." 2020. FilmRatings.com. https://www.filmratings.com/Content/Downloads/rating_rules.pdf.

6 Ibid

7 "Strong's Hebrew: 7723. אָוְשׁ (shav) — emptiness, vanity." n.d. Bible Hub. Accessed December 27, 2022. https://biblehub.com/hebrew/7723.htm.

8 "Blasphemy Definition & Meaning." 2022. Merriam-Webster. https://www.merriam-webster.com/dictionary/blasphemy. Accessed December 19, 2022.

9 Nalkur PG, Jamieson PE, Romer D. The effectiveness of the motion picture association of America's rating system in screening explicit violence and sex in top-ranked movies from 1950 to 2006. J Adolesc Health. 2010 Nov;47(5):440-7. doi: 10.1016/j.jadohealth.2010.01.019. Epub 2010 Apr 2. PMID: 20970078.

10 Lin WH, Liu CH, Yi CC. Exposure to sexually explicit media in early adolescence is related to risky sexual behavior in emerging adulthood. PLoS One. 2020 Apr 10;15(4):e0230242. doi: 10.1371/journal.pone.0230242. PMID: 32275669; PMCID: PMC7147756.

11 "How ad spending in the US compares to the rest of the world." 2022. Wicked Reports. https://www.wickedreports.com/blog/how-ad-spending-in-the-us-compares-to-the-rest-of-the-world.

Chapter 5

1 "Modest definition and meaning | Collins English Dictionary." n.d. Collins Dictionary. Accessed January 19, 2023. https://www.collinsdictionary.com/us/dictionary/english/modest.

2 Butt, Sheila K. 2002. Seeking Spiritual Beauty. N.p.22: Publishing Designs, Incorporated.

3 Ibid

4 "Visitation FAQs." n.d. GDC. Accessed January 24, 2023. https://gdc.ga.gov/sites/default/files/Visitation_FAQs_0.pdf.

5 Hamann S, Herman RA, Nolan CL, Wallen K. Men and women differ in amygdala response to visual sexual stimuli. Nat Neurosci. 2004 Apr;7(4):411-6. doi: 10.1038/nn1208. Epub 2004 Mar 7. PMID: 15004563.

6 Camilleri C, Perry JT, Sammut S. Compulsive Internet Pornography Use and Mental Health: A Cross-Sectional Study in a Sample

of University Students in the United States. Front Psychol. 2021 Jan 12;11:613244. doi: 10.3389/fpsyg.2020.613244. PMID: 33510691; PMCID: PMC7835260.

7 Balmet, Jami. 2014. "What Modesty is {and isn't}: A Practical Approach." https://findingjoyinyourhome.com/what-modesty-is-and-isnt/

8 "Loincloth - Facts and History of Loincloth." n.d. History of Clothing. Accessed January 25, 2023. http://www.historyofclothing.com/clothing-history/loincloth/.

9 "Kethoneth – Bible Clothing." n.d. Bible Clothing. Accessed January 25, 2023. https://www.bibleclothing.com/hebrew-garments/inner-garments/kethoneth/.

10 "Tunic Definition & Meaning." 2023. Merriam-Webster. https://www.merriam-webster.com/dictionary/tunic.

11 Moorman, Chloe, Jamie Oliver, Jillian Stacy, Makenzi Oliver, and Holland Stacy. 2021. Fearfully and Wonderfully Made: A Teen Girl's Guide to Growing in Christ. N.p.3: Focus Press, Incorporated.

12 Sobotta, Johannes. n.d. "Anatomy, Bony Pelvis and Lower Limb, Anterior Thigh Muscles." NCBI. Accessed January 25, 2023. https://www.ncbi.nlm.nih.gov/books/NBK538425/.

13 "Encyclopaedia Britannica's Great Inventions". Encyclopaedia Britannica. Archived from the original on 5 January 2007. Accessed January 26, 2023.

14 "Is Modesty a Thing of the Past?" 2014. Censor This! https://ksscensorthis.com/1831/opinion/is-modesty-a-thing-of-the-past/. Accessed January 26, 2023.

Chapter 6

1 "Teens, Social Media and Technology 2022." 2022. Pew Research Center. https://www.pewresearch.org/internet/2022/08/10/teens-social-media-and-technology-2022/.

2 "Media Use by Tweens and Teens: Infographic." n.d. Common Sense Media. Accessed February 7, 2023. https://www.commonsensemedia.org/the-common-sense-census-media-use-by-tweens-and-teens-infographic.

3 Wheelwright, Trevor. 2022. "2022 Cell Phone Usage Statistics: How Obsessed Are We?" Reviews.org. https://www.reviews.org/mobile/cell-phone-addiction/.

4 Brodersen, Kayla, Nour Hammami, and Tarun Reddy Katapally. 2022. "Smartphone Use and Mental Health among Youth: It Is Time to Develop Smartphone-Specific Screen Time Guidelines" Youth 2, no. 1: 23-38. https://doi.org/10.3390/youth2010003

5 Kardaras, Nicholas. 2017. Glow Kids: How Screen Addiction Is Hijacking Our Kids—and How to Break the Trance. N.p.4: St. Martin's Publishing Group.

6 Palmer, James. 2021. "Why China Is Cracking Down on Video Games." Foreign Policy. https://foreignpolicy.com/2021/09/01/china-video-game-online-crackdown/.

7 Siegel, Daniel J., and Tina P. Bryson. 2011. The Whole-Brain Child: 12 Revolutionary Strategies to Nurture Your Child's Developing Mind. N.p.38: Random House Publishing Group.

8 "Brainstem: Overview, Function & Anatomy." n.d. Cleveland Clinic. Accessed February 4, 2023. https://my.clevelandclinic.org/health/body/21598-brainstem.

9 Siegel, Daniel J., and Tina P. Bryson. 2011. The Whole-Brain Child: 12 Revolutionary Strategies to Nurture Your Child's Developing Mind. N.p.39: Random House Publishing Group.

10 "Sarah-Jayne Blakemore: The mysterious workings of the adolescent brain." 2012. YouTube. https://www.youtube.com/watch?v=6zVS8HIPUng.

11 Gary W. Small, Jooyeon Lee, Aaron Kaufman, Jason Jalil, Prabha Siddarth, Himaja Gaddipati, Teena D. Moody & Susan Y. Bookheimer (2020) Brain health consequences of digital technology

use , Dialogues in Clinical Neuroscience, 22:2, 179-187, DOI: 10.31887/DCNS.2020.22.2/gsmall

12 Ibid

13 Kardaras, Nicholas. 2017. Glow Kids: How Screen Addiction Is Hijacking Our Kids—and How to Break the Trance. N.p.21: St. Martin's Publishing Group.

14 "Dopamine, Smartphones & You: A battle for your time." 2018. Science in the News. https://sitn.hms.harvard.edu/flash/2018/dopamine-smartphones-battle-time/.

15 "Digital Trends & Social Media Statistics 2022 October Update." n.d. Hootsuite. Accessed February 18, 2023. https://www.hootsuite.com/resources/digital-trends-q4-update.

16 "Teens, Social Media and Technology 2022." 2022. Pew Research Center. https://www.pewresearch.org/internet/2022/08/10/teens-social-media-and-technology-2022/.

17 Digital Trends & Social Media.

18 Kardaras, Nicholas. 2017. Glow Kids: How Screen Addiction Is Hijacking Our Kids—and How to Break the Trance. N.p.83: St. Martin's Publishing Group.

19 Hari, Johann. "This could be why you're depressed or anxious." 2019. TED. https://www.youtube.com/watch?v=MB5IX-np5fE

20 Bowler, Abby. 2020. "Isolation Among Generation Z in the United States." BYU ScholarsArchive. https://scholarsarchive.byu.edu/cgi/viewcontent.cgi?article=1059&context=ballardbrief.

21 "Youth Risk Behavior Survey Data Summary & Trends Report: 2011-2021." n.d. CDC. Accessed February 16, 2023. https://www.cdc.gov/healthyyouth/data/yrbs/pdf/YRBS_Data-Summary-Trends_Report2023_508.pdf. Add 2023 data

22 Bowler, Abby. 2020. "Isolation Among Generation Z in the United States." BYU ScholarsArchive. https://scholarsarchive.byu.edu/cgi/viewcontent.cgi?article=1059&context=ballardbrief.

23 Shrier, Abigail. 2021. Irreversible Damage: The Transgender Craze Seducing Our Daughters. N.p.3: Regnery Publishing.

24 Kardaras, Nicholas. 2017. Glow Kids: How Screen Addiction Is Hijacking Our Kids—and How to Break the Trance. N.p.91: St. Martin's Publishing Group.

25 Tegano, Rachel. 2022. "Nonverbal Communication in the Workplace: the Secret to Team Trust." BetterUp. https://www.betterup.com/blog/the-secret-to-building-trust-lies-in-the-unspoken?hsLang=en.

26 Hari, Johann. "Everything You Think You Know About Addiction Is Wrong."2015.TED. https://www.youtube.com/watch?v=PY9DcIMGxMs&t=1s.

27 Kardaras. Glow Kids. Appendix.

28 "Screen Time and Children." n.d. AACAP. Accessed February 18, 2023. https://www.aacap.org/AACAP/Families_and_Youth/Facts_for_Families/FFF-Guide/Children-And-Watching-TV-054.aspx.

29 n.d. Canadian 24-Hour Movement Guidelines: 24-Hour Movement Guidelines. Accessed February 17, 2023. https://csepguidelines.ca/.

30 Nakshine V S, Thute P, Khatib M, et al. (October 08, 2022) Increased Screen Time as a Cause of Declining Physical, Psychological Health, and Sleep Patterns: A Literary Review. Cureus 14(10): e30051. doi:10.7759/cureus.30051

31 Zhao, Yihong, Martin Paulus, Kara S. Bagot, R. Todd Constable, H. Klar Yaggi, Nancy S. Redeker, and Marc N. Potenza. "Brain structural covariation linked to screen media activity and externalizing behaviors in children," Journal of Behavioral Addictions 11, 2 (2022): 417-426, doi: https://doi.org/10.1556/2006.2022.00044

Chapter 7

1 "The 2022 Year In Review." Pornhub Insights.8 December 2022. https://www.pornhub.com/insights/2022-year-in-review Accessed 13 March 2023.

2 Ballester-Arnal, R., García-Barba, M., Castro-Calvo, J. et al. Pornography Consumption in People of Different Age Groups: an Analysis Based on Gender, Contents, and Consequences. Sex Res Soc Policy (2022). https://doi.org/10.1007/s13178-022-00720-z

3 Madigan S, Ly A, Rash CL, Van Ouytsel J, Temple JR. Prevalence of Multiple Forms of Sexting Behavior Among Youth: A Systematic Review and Meta-analysis. JAMA Pediatr. 2018;172(4):327–335. doi:10.1001/jamapediatrics.2017.5314

4 "The 2022 Year In Review". Pornhub Insights. 8 December 2022. https://www.pornhub.com/insights/2022-year-in-review Accessed 13 March 2023.

5 "3 Ways Bark Protects Your Child from Porn." Defend Young Minds™, 25 August 2020, https://www.defendyoungminds.com/post/3-ways-bark-protects-your-child-from-porn. Accessed 9 March 2023.

6 Anne, Maheux J., et al. "Associations between adolescents' pornography consumption and self-objectification, body comparison, and body shame." https://doi.org/10.1016/j.bodyim.2021.01.014, 01 06 2021, https://www.sciencedirect.com/science/article/pii/S1740144521000140. Accessed 09 March 2023

7 Robb, M.B., & Mann, S. (2023). Teens and pornography. San Francisco, CA: Common Sense.

https://www.commonsensemedia.org/sites/default/files/research/report/2022-teens-and-pornography-final-web.pdf.

8 "2014 Year in Review." Porn Hub Insights. 7 January 2015. https://www.pornhub.com/insights/2014-year-in-review Accessed 14 March 2023.

9 "The 2022 Year In Review." Pornhub Insights. 8 December 2022. https://www.pornhub.com/insights/2022-year-in-review Accessed 13 March 2023.

10 Robb, M.B., & Mann, S. (2023). Teens and pornography. San Francisco, CA: Common Sense. https://www.commonsensemedia. org/sites/default/files/research/report/2022-teens-and-pornography-final-web.pdf.

11 Martellozzo, Elena; Monaghan, Andy; Adler, Joanna R; Davidson, Julia; Leyva, Rodolfo; Horvath, Miranda A H (2017): "I wasn't sure it was normal to watch it." figshare. Dataset. https://doi.org/10.6084/m9.figshare.3382393.v4

12 https://www.covenanteyes.com/2014/02/03/brain-chemicals-and-porn-addiction/

13 Camilleri C, Perry JT, Sammut S. Compulsive Internet Pornography Use and Mental Health: A Cross-Sectional Study in a Sample of University Students in the United States. Front Psychol. 2021 Jan 12;11:613244. doi: 10.3389/fpsyg.2020.613244. PMID: 33510691; PMCID: PMC7835260.

14 Fight the New Drug. "How Porn Can Become An Escalating Behavior." 2023. https://fightthenewdrug.org/how-porn-can-become-an-escalating-behavior/ Accessed 13 March 2023.

15 Owens, Candice. "The Normalization of Incestuous Porn and What It Means for America." Episode 2. 13 September, 2022. The Daily Wire Podcast.

16 Fratti, Karen. "Why sexting is something you should definitely do in a relationship." HelloGiggles, 4 April 2018, https://hellogiggles. com/why-sexting-is-something-you-should-definitely-do-in-a-relationship/. Accessed 10 March 2023.

17 Martellozzo, "I wasn't sure it was normal."

18 Mohiyeddini, Changiz, and William Beaumont. 2021. "Compulsive Internet Pornography Use and Mental Health: A Cross-Sectional Study in a Sample of University Students in the United States." NCBI. https://www.ncbi.nlm.nih.gov/pmc/articles/PMC7835260/.

19 Arterburn, Stephen, Fred Stoeker, and Mike Yorkey. 2009. Every Young Man's Battle: Strategies for Victory in the Real World of Sexual Temptation. N.p.140: Crown Publishing Group.

Chapter 8

1 Sherri Hill 2023. https://www.sherrihill.com/blog/best-prom-dresses-that-will-make.html

2 Rupp HA, Wallen K. Sex differences in response to visual sexual stimuli: a review. Arch Sex Behav. 2008 Apr;37(2):206-18. doi: 10.1007/s10508-007-9217-9. Epub 2007 Aug 1. PMID: 17668311; PMCID: PMC2739403.

3 Aran, Isha. 2016. "Do teens ACTUALLY lose their virginity on prom night?" Splinter News. https://splinternews.com/do-teens-actually-lose-their-virginity-on-prom-night-1793856371.

4 Barker, Tess. 2015. "Why Prom Is (Probably) The Wrong Night To Lose Your Virginity." MTV. https://www.mtv.com/news/qrh2jq/lose-virginity-prom.

5 Plante, Chandler, and Kathleen H. Owens. 2020. "Want to Have Sex on Prom Night? Here's How to Prepare." POPSUGAR. https://www.popsugar.com/love/things-to-know-before-losing-your-virginity-47211777.

6 "Skip the Prom and Go Straight to the After Party." Promnightlife.com. Accessed 11 April 2023. https://promnightlife.com/blog/skip-prom-straight-after-party

7 Spurgeon, CH. n.d. "G766 - aselgeia - Strong's Greek Lexicon (nasb20)." Blue Letter Bible. Accessed March 29, 2023. https://www.blueletterbible.org/lexicon/g766/nasb20/tr/0-1/.

8 Wright, C.L., & Craske, M. (2015). Music's Influence on Risky Sexual Behaviors: Examining the Cultivation Theory. Media Psychology Review. Vol. 9(1)

Chapter 9

1 Owens, Candace. The Candace Owens Show. "Why I Am Not an 'Ally' to the Gay Community." 19 April 2023.

2 Ballinger, Chris. "JoJo Siwa On Her Decision to Come Out and Falling In Love With Her New Girlfriend | PEOPLE." YouTube, 7 April 2021, https://www.youtube.com/watch?v=7oD0v9qXJps. Accessed 21 April 2023.

3 "How Many Adults and Youth Identify as Transgender in the United States?" June 2022. Williams Institute, https://williamsinstitute.law.ucla.edu/publications/trans-adults-united-states/. Accessed 21 April 2023.

4 Gomez, Ronnie, and step guide. "Full YouTube Statistics Checklist for 2023." Sprout Social, 28 February 2023, https://sproutsocial.com/insights/youtube-stats/. Accessed 21 April 2023.

5 "Psychiatry.org—What is Gender Dysphoria?" American Psychiatric Association, https://www.psychiatry.org/patients-families/gender-dysphoria/what-is-gender-dysphoria. Accessed 20 April 2023.

6 Littman, Lisa. "Parent reports of adolescents and young adults perceived to show signs of a rapid onset of gender dysphoria." PLOS, 16 August 2018, https://journals.plos.org/plosone/article?id=10.1371/journal.pone.0202330. Accessed 21 April 2023.

7 Shrier, Abigail. Irreversible Damage: The Transgender Craze Seducing Our Daughters. p. xxvii Regnery Publishing, 2021.

8 Ibid, p. xxvii

9 Ibid, p. xxvii

10 "US Population by Year." S&P 500 PE Ratio. Accessed May 6, 2023. https://www.multpl.com/united-states-population/table/by-year; RESPAUT, ROBIN, and CHAD TERHUNE. 2022. "Number of transgender children seeking treatment surges in U.S." Reuters. https://www.reuters.com/investigates/special-report/usa-transyouth-data/.

11 Flores, Andrew, Herman, Jody L. & Kathryn K O'Neill. June 2022. "How Many Adults and Youth Identify as Transgender in the United States?" n.d. Williams Institute. Accessed April 21, 2023. https://williamsinstitute.law.ucla.edu/publications/trans-adults-united-states/.

12 Psychiatry.org—What is Gender Dysphoria?" American Psychiatric Association, https://www.psychiatry.org/patients-families/gender-dysphoria/what-is-gender-dysphoria. Accessed 20 April 2023.

13 Arden, Chloe. 5/1/2023. "100 Transgender YouTube Channels on Transgender Transition and Life Experience Videos." Feedspot Blog. Accessed May 2, 2023. https://blog.feedspot.com/transgender_youtube_channels/.

14 "shane." May 1, 2023. YouTube. Accessed May 2, 2023. https://www.youtube.com/@shane/about; "James Charles." May 1, 2023. YouTube. Accessed May 2, 2023. https://www.youtube.com/@JamesCharles/about.

15 Shrier, Abigail. Irreversible Damage: The Transgender Craze Seducing Our Daughters. p.45.Regnery Publishing, 2021.

16 "I Think I Might Be Transgender." Advocates for Youth, https://www.advocatesforyouth.org/wp-content/uploads/2019/03/ITIMB-Trans-for-print.pdf. Accessed 24 April 2023.

17 Stanford, Libby, and Ronen Tivony. 2022. "Biden's Order on LGBTQ Equality: What Educators Need to Know." Education Week. https://www.edweek.org/leadership/bidens-order-on-lgbtq-equality-what-educators-need-to-know/2022/06.

18 Overton, Heidi, and Alexandra Campana. 2023. "Gender Transition Medications and Surgeries for Children in the U.S." America First Policy Institute. https://americafirstpolicy.com/issues/gender-transition-medications-and-surgeries-for-children-in-the-u.s.

19 Wylie C Hembree, Peggy T Cohen-Kettenis, Louis Gooren, Sabine E Hannema, Walter J Meyer, M Hassan Murad, Stephen M Rosenthal, Joshua D Safer, Vin Tangpricha, Guy G T'Sjoen, Endocrine Treatment of Gender-Dysphoric/Gender-Incongruent Persons: An Endocrine Society Clinical Practice Guideline, The Journal of Clinical Endocrinology & Metabolism, Volume 102, Issue 11, 1 November 2017, Pages 3869–3903, https://doi.org/10.1210/jc.2017-01658

20 "20:20 My Secret Self Complete Documentary." 2016. YouTube. https://www.youtube.com/watch?v=eJ_BHY5RolA.

21 Ibid

22 Substance Abuse and Mental Health Services Administration (SAMHSA): Moving Beyond Change Efforts: Evidence and Action to Support and Affirm LGBTQI+ Youth. SAMHSA Publication No. PEP22 03-12-001. Rockville, MD: Center for Substance Abuse Prevention. Substance Abuse and Mental Health Services Administration, 2023.

23 Fielding J, Bass C. Individuals seeking gender reassignment: marked increase in demand for services. BJPsych Bull. 2018 Oct;42(5):206-210. doi: 10.1192/bjp.2018.30. Epub 2018 Jun 12. PMID: 29893661; PMCID: PMC6189985.

24 Block J. Gender dysphoria in young people is rising—and so is professional disagreement BMJ 2023; 380 :p382 doi:10.1136/bmj.p382

25 "A Sad Confessional By Jazz Jennings." 2023. YouTube. https://www.youtube.com/watch?v=U2lmlWy0yXg.

26 "Transgender Kids—Who Knows Best—BBC Documentary Banned in Canada." 2018. Vimeo. https://vimeo.com/256415639.

27 Johnston, Jeff. September 13, 2015. "Transgenderism: Blurring the Lines." Focus on the Family. https://www.focusonthefamily.com/get-help/transgenderism-blurring-the-lines/.

28 Sims, Andrew. "Biblical View on Transgender Identity: A Primer for Parents and Strugglers." Focus on the Family. Accessed May 3, 2023. https://www.focusonthefamily.com/parenting/a-biblical-perspective-on-transgender-identity-a-primer-for-parents-and-strugglers/.

29 Thomas, Gary, Danny Huerta, and Andrew Sims. "Biblical View on Transgender Identity: A Primer for Parents and Strugglers." Focus on the Family. Accessed May 3, 2023. https://www.focusonthefamily. com/parenting/a-biblical-perspective-on-transgender-identity-a-primer-for-parents-and-strugglers/.

30 Defending the Faith Study Bible. 2019. p.1735-1736: Apologetics Press.

Chapter 10

1 Brown, Anna. 2020. "Americans' Views on Dating and Relationships." Pew Research Center. https://www.pewresearch.org/social-trends/2020/08/20/nearly-half-of-u-s-adults-say-dating-has-gotten-harder-for-most-people-in-the-last-10-years/.

2 Martinez, Gladys M., and Joyce C. Abma. 2020. "Products - Data Briefs - Number 366 - May 2020." Centers for Disease Control and Prevention. https://www.cdc.gov/nchs/products/databriefs/db366.htm.

3 Previtera, Petrelli. 2023. "Divorce Statistics for 2022 in the US." Petrelli Previtera, LLC. https://www.petrellilaw.com/divorce-statistics-for-2022/.

4 Heffernan, Carol, and Gary Thomas. n.d. "God's design for marriage." Focus on the Family Canada. Accessed June 20, 2023. https://www.focusonthefamily.ca/content/gods-design-for-marriage.

5 Ibid

6 "Oxytocin." n.d. Psychology Today. Accessed June 20, 2023. https://www.psychologytoday.com/us/basics/oxytocin.

7 Gresh, Dannah. 2004. And the Bride Wore White: Seven Secrets to Sexual Purity. N.p.90: Moody Publishers.

8 Ibid., 91

9 Pastor Kj. 2011. I Hear You God….but HOW? N.p.84: XULON Press.

10 Gresh, Dannah, p. 64-66

Chapter 11

1 "I Am Meth." Speak Up Against Meth. Accessed August 2, 2023. https://methproject.org/speak/1313-i-am-meth.html.

2 "Louisiana mom finds voice through TikTok after drunk driver kills kids." 2023. USA Today. https://www.usatoday.com/story/news/nation/2023/06/19/tiktok-mom-3-kids-killed-drunk-driver/70322589007/.

3 Ibid

4 Hawkins, Sally. 2019. "Teen who was put on life-support for vaping says 'I didn't think of myself as a smoker.'" ABC News. https://abcnews.go.com/US/teen-put-life-support-vaping-didnt-smoker/story?id=65522370.

5 Ibid

6 "Most reported substance use among adolescents held steady in 2022 | National Institute on Drug Abuse." 2022. National Institute on Drug Abuse. https://nida.nih.gov/news-events/news-releases/2022/12/most-reported-substance-use-among-adolescents-held-steady-in-2022.

7 Cooper, et al. Vaping Misperceptions. MMWR 2022. Center for Tobacco Products. www.fda.gov/tobacco

8 "Teen Vaping." n.d. Smokefree Teen. Accessed August 8, 2023. https://teen.smokefree.gov/therealcost

9 "Quick Facts on the Risks of E-cigarettes for Young People." November 10, 2022. CDC. Accessed August 8, 2023. https://www.cdc.gov/tobacco/basic_information/e-cigarettes/Quick-Facts-on-the-Risks-of-E-cigarettes-for-Kids-Teens-and-Young-Adults.html?s_cid=OSH_emg_GL0001.

10 Cooper, et al. Vaping Misperceptions. MMWR 2022. Center for Tobacco Products. www.fda.gov/tobacco

11 "The Risks of Vaping." May 2023. U.S. Food & Drug Administration.

12 Ibid

13 Adrienne R. Hughes, Sara Grusing, Amber Lin, Robert G. Hendrickson, David C. Sheridan, Rebecca Marshall & B. Zane Horowitz (2023) Trends in intentional abuse and misuse ingestions in school-aged children and adolescents reported to US poison centers from 2000-2020, Clinical Toxicology, 61:1, 64-71, DOI: 10.1080/15563650.2022.2120818

14 NIDA. Cannabis.

15 "Teens | Health Effects | Marijuana." 2021. CDC. https://www.cdc.gov/marijuana/health-effects/teens.html.

16 NIDA. 2019, December 24. Cannabis (Marijuana) DrugFacts. Retrieved from https://nida.nih.gov/publications/drugfacts/cannabis-marijuana on 2023, August 10.

17 "Mental Health | Health Effects | Marijuana." 2020. CDC. https://www.cdc.gov/marijuana/health-effects/mental-health.html.

18 Michael S. Gilson, Jason R. Kilmer, Christine M. Lee, Mary E. Larimer, Prom, graduation and parties: Alcohol use and normative perceptions among high school seniors during specific events, Addictive Behaviors, Volume 138,2023, 107569, ISSN 0306-4603, https://doi.org/10.1016/j.addbeh.2022.107569.

19 "Consequences for Families in the United States." 2023. National Institute on Alcohol Abuse and Alcoholism (NIAAA). Accessed August 7, 2023. https://www.niaaa.nih.gov/alcohols-effects-health/alcohol-topics/alcohol-facts-and-statistics/consequences-families-united-states.

20 "Excessive Alcohol Use." 2022. CDC. https://www.cdc.gov/chronicdisease/resources/publications/factsheets/alcohol.htm.

21 "Alcohol and the Human Body." n.d. National Institute on

Alcohol Abuse and Alcoholism (NIAAA). Accessed August 7, 2023. https://www.niaaa.nih.gov/alcohols-effects-health/alcohol-topics/alcohol-facts-and-statistics/alcohol-and-human-body.

22 McCarthy, Claire. 2021. "Alcohol harms the brain in teen years—before and after that, too." Harvard Health. https://www.health.harvard.edu/blog/alcohol-harms-the-brain-in-teen-years-before-and-after-that-too-2021011521758.

23 Fitzgerald, Scott. n.d. "Quote by F. Scott Fitzgerald: "First you take a drink, then the drink takes a ...""" Goodreads. Accessed August 11, 2023. https://www.goodreads.com/quotes/4738-first-you-take-a-drink-then-the-drink-takes-a.

24 "Cannabis (Marijuana) and Cannabinoids: What You Need To Know." November 2019. National Center for Complementary and Integrative Health. Accessed August 14, 2023. https://www.nccih.nih.gov/health/cannabis-marijuana-and-cannabinoids-what-you-need-to-know.

25 "I Am Meth." Speak Up Against Meth. Accessed August 2, 2023. https://methproject.org/speak/1313-i-am-meth.html.

Chapter 12

1 Wilson, Sandra D. 1993. Hurt People Hurt People: Hope & Healing for Yourself and Your Relationships. N.p.: T. Nelson.

2 "Alan Redpath Quote: THINK before you speak. Is it True, Helpful, Inspiring, Necessary, Kind?" n.d. Minimalist Quotes. Accessed August 24, 2023. https://minimalistquotes.com/alan-redpath-quote-263217/.

Chapter 13

1 "16 Interesting Facts About Pearls - TPS Blog." n.d. The Pearl Source. Accessed September 27, 2023. https://www.thepearlsource.com/blog/pearl-facts-beautiful-organic-essence-pearls/.

2 Ward, Fred. 1998. "The History of Pearls | NOVA." PBS. https://www.pbs.org/wgbh/nova/article/history-pearls/.

3 Gresh, Dannah. 2004. And the Bride Wore White: Seven Secrets to Sexual Purity. p.107: Moody Publishers.

4 Tant, Jefferson D., and Bruce Edwards. 2022. "Thoughts on Baptism – La Vista Church of Christ." La Vista Church of Christ. https://www.lavistachurchofchrist.org/cms/thoughts-on-baptism/.

5 Gresh, Dannah. 2004. And the Bride Wore White: Seven Secrets to Sexual Purity. p.106-110: Moody Publishers.